Stellar Observations fr

Because hunger is a significant issue bold leadership and innovative solutions are required. Food is among the most elemental human needs and addressing food insecurity directly impacts the success of our other societal challenges, allowing individuals to work, learn, raise their families and age with the health, dignity and respect they deserve. Jan and Colleen's combined talents grew the North Texas Food Bank (NTFB) into a leading impact organization which currently provides over 70 million nutritious meals annually and aims to provide 92 million by 2025. Colleen's journey, as explained in her book, is intimate and engaging, and explains the source of her passion for both helping those at the front lines as well as inviting others to join the mission.

Katherine Perot Reeves
Civic Leader
NTFB Board of Directors, Since 2011
Honorary Co-Chair, *Stop Hunger Build Hope* NTFB Capital Campaign

You seem to have discovered, like your parents, the elusive meaning of life. Through your genuine relationships, your belief that every life has equal value, and your commitment to improving the lives of so many, I truly believe you have found it.

Pam Beckert
Civic Leader
Co-Chair, *Stop Hunger Build Hope* NTFB Capital Campaign

While Colleen and I first grew our friendship during our 2010 Leadership Women class, working alongside her during my first six months as CEO of the Food Bank was priceless. Her passion, determination against all odds and servant leadership played a pivotal role in the achievement of our historic $55 million campaign and growing the NTFB brand over her sixteen years there. Her retirement is well deserved. Colleen's candid insights and personal stories build a case study applicable to any organization seeking transformational change. A must-read for board members, executive staff and external-facing team members.

Trisha Cunningham
President & CEO, NTFB

Passion and professionalism define Colleen. I was inspired as I worked collaboratively with her and her team in our endeavor to feed thousands of chronically hungry children. I could not have been prouder of our efforts and appreciated Colleen and the North Texas Food Bank's guidance each step of the way.

Mayor Harry LaRosiliere
City of Plano, Texas

A powerful story of leadership by two, with endurance and achievement amid incredible challenges. A must-read for anyone in business or nonprofit, especially if you're about to launch your moonshot journey. What happened at the North Texas Food Bank is as remarkable as planting your flag on Everest without the aid of a compass.

Anurag Jain
Chairman, Access Healthcare
Chairman, NTFB Board of Directors, 2017–2019

Charged with a record-setting capital campaign goal and faced with personal adversity throughout the campaign, Colleen truly exemplified grace under pressure. With a great deal of passion and commitment, she makes known in her writing that anyone can instill change. The story of her experience working with the North Texas Food Bank is a valuable road map for those who wish to begin a nonprofit journey of their own.

Thomas E. Black, Jr.
Black, Mann & Graham, L.L.P.
Chairman, NTFB Board of Directors, 2013–2017

I believe this book is an excellent tool for any executive director, development director or board of directors requiring exponential growth to meet the challenging needs of the communities they serve. Within the context of an amazing story, Colleen provides valuable insights and a clear road map to building a resilient brand. Colleen is an inspiration within the Food Bank community and beyond.

Lydia Chase
Civic Leader
Member, NTFB Capital Campaign Committee

Her story from Battery Lane to NTFB illustrates how Colleen has built and lived her remarkable life based on the five leadership traits. Over a decade, I have witnessed her 'Authenticity' in dealing with people and her purpose, her 'Collaborative' attitude within the community at large, her 'Intelligence' through discussions, her 'Bold vision' in defining the unsurmountable three-year capital campaign, and her 'Being opportunistic' in seeking opportunity to help others. I have always appreciated her positive attitude toward life, her nature of always helping anyone and everyone, and her connecting people through her relationships for greater good. Her relentless pursuit of reaching her three-year capital campaign goal could only be achieved through the moonshot leadership she demonstrated and by using the concepts she has so easily laid out in her book, the *Char Minars* and "leadership by two."

Gurvendra S. Suri
Founder and CEO, The Suri Group; Chairman, AST Corporation
Board Member, Stratix Corporation and Core BTS
Founder, Beyond Borders

Colleen is one of the rarest breeds in the nonprofit fundraising community that I have known. She has the following traits that have led to her stellar career and results at the NTFB: she is fearless, yet caring; graciously calculating, yet ambitious; she is confident and driven for the purpose of the mission, yet genuine and human in her fundraising efforts—all of which are a terrific combination of talents that culminated in the completion of the Food Bank's $55 million capital campaign. She has well deserved her formal retirement. The NTFB would not have obtained the many levels of its fundraising success without Colleen.

Ray Hemmig
Founder, Retail & Restaurant Growth Capital
Former Chairman, NTFB Board of Directors

While success comes to a team, every team needs a coach. Every bus needs a driver; every plane needs a pilot. For the North Texas Food Bank's marketing, that leader has been Colleen Townsley Brinkmann. There is a view that each of us at work is the average of the five people we spend the most time with. For the Food Bank's marketing and fundraising teams, one of those folks is likely Colleen—and they have been fortunate—even though Colleen would never say that about herself.

Jack Phifer
Chief Marketing Officer, Moroch (retired)

I first met Colleen when she called on me with Jan Pruitt on behalf of the North Texas Food Bank and was impressed with her passion from the moment we met. Colleen has been an integral part of the NTFB culture since she joined them and I consider her contribution invaluable to the organization.

Jay Pack
Pack Group; Former Chairman, NTFB Board of Directors

It is most rare to find a book that encompasses two such rarely combined messages. One of a bold, strategic business plan to raise $55 million, and one of a heartwarming tale of two bold, courageous women whose friendship and determination took them across the finish line. This book is a lesson to be learned for the nonprofit world and an inspiring challenge for us to look inside ourselves to do something that really matters in this life. Colleen's greatest asset is her love for others—love conquers all.

Connie Yates
Tom Thumb & Albertsons Public Affairs
Former Member, NTFB Board of Directors

Colleen is a natural born leader, communicator and connector with a background that exhibits inclusion, diversity and tremendous care and concern for her fellow man, woman and child. It was an honor to work with her at the North Texas Food Bank, as the universal elements of transformational change were truly on display in "making good happen" and changing the world through her set of "internal convictions." Janie and I say thank you and job well done.

Preston Pearson
Five-time Super Bowl Participant with two Championships
Baltimore Colts, Pittsburgh Steelers, Dallas Cowboys

Colleen truly exemplifies a servant leader. The life lessons she presents in this book are essential for anyone who wants to have an impact in their community.

Chad Hennings
Three-time Super Bowl Champion, Dallas Cowboys
Founder, Wingmen Ministries

I have had the pleasure and privilege of working with Colleen and the North Texas Food Bank for over five years and there are always two things that I come away with from my encounters—total committed passion for the cause and absolute belief in the team's ability to meet the challenge. This, coupled with the competence and professionalism of the leadership team, has produced the tremendous results that Colleen refers to in the attached pages. I would strongly recommend this as required reading for anyone who wants to learn how she helped build the best brand in North Texas: the North Texas Food Bank.

Shaun Mara
Chief Financial Officer, Dean Foods & Atkins Nutritionals
NTFB Board of Directors, 2012 – Present

Bringing the best of the heart and the head is what makes someone successful in philanthropic endeavors. I have not come across anyone who does this with more ease and aplomb than Colleen. Her book and experiences are like a masterclass to not only those who want to succeed in philanthropy, but also those who want to make a real impact on communities. Thanks to Colleen's magnanimous worldview, I see her already creating the multiplier effect through her new efforts and collaborative spirit.

Venky Raghavendra,
Vice President of Advancement, Safe Water Network
Ambassador & Thought Leader, American India Foundation

Colleen brings an unmatched commitment to achieving every goal. Her fundraising acumen and successes should be a road map for every nonprofit.

Joyce Goss
Executive Director, The Goss-Michael Foundation

How wonderful of Colleen to share the story of how the needle was moved in fighting hunger in North Texas! Her inspiration, ideas, incredible teamwork with Jan, and the well-oiled team of staff, volunteers and board members brought the community together like never before to make a huge impact on an issue that will cause a positive ripple effect. I am so glad Jan thought big and that Colleen was there to continue to create and help make the plan to use food distribution hubs, boost the volume capacities and infrastructure of food pantries, and reduce costs a reality. I hope other communities will follow many of these ideas and the ripple effect will continue.

Sarah Losinger
Trustee, John R. McCune Charitable Trust

I was privileged to meet Colleen during my terms as board member and chair of the Greater Dallas Community of Churches. It has been personally rewarding to see her "find her shine" there and in subsequent roles, culminating with a successful career at the North Texas Food Bank. More than a fundraiser, Colleen is the ultimate "friend-raiser," and nonprofit leaders and volunteers are well advised to take note of her story.

Ruben E. Esquivel
Vice President, Community and Corporate Relations
UT Southwestern Medical Center

Colleen is an exceptional, mission-driven leader. In my role as a foundation executive, I've always found her to be thoughtful and strategic, but her ability to mentor others is what really makes her effective.

Brent E. Christopher
President, Children's Medical Center Foundation

I would highly recommend this *compelling, must-read* leadership book which is packed full of valuable and meaningful insights and advice for all leaders, beyond nonprofit. This book will re-inspire you and reinvigorate you and your thoughts of your personal leadership style and journey. I had the great pleasure of watching Colleen's leadership in action while I served on the NTFB Board during one of the most impactful and transformational times in the Food Bank's history. Leveraging her unwavering tenacity and tremendous passion for the cause and our stakeholders, she launched a significant capital campaign; and during that time, we lost our fearless long-tenured CEO leader who passed away. However, thanks to Colleen's leadership, reputation in the community and dedication, we were able to achieve our goal and onboard a new CEO at the same time. An amazing feat by an amazing leader!

Kim Warmbier
CHRO, Sabre
Former Member, NTFB Board of Directors

Colleen is absolutely the most passionate social entrepreneur I have ever met. Her desire to end food insecurity was like nothing I have ever seen and her strategies on how to do it have proven to be spot on. Watching and working with Colleen has been one of the biggest treats of my life.

Mitch Fadel
CEO, Rent-A-Center, Inc.
Former Member, NTFB Board of Directors

Moonshot Leadership tells a compelling story of bringing inspiration and sustainable solutions to address hunger. A must-read for anyone interested in leadership and making a real difference in the world.

Brad Sanders
Co-CEO, Raising Cane's Chicken Fingers

Colleen notes that justice and compassion were embedded into her (and her sister's) DNA. "Embedded" is an understatement—justice and compassion have defined her life during the thirty years I have known her. She has made a profoundly positive mark on North Texas, both as a former television producer and as an executive plotting the growth and success of the North Texas Food Bank. Colleen's service to our entire community (especially those without means) has been an inspiration to my family. I am confident that this book will serve to motivate us to do more for our communities and provide us with lessons and skills to fulfill our missions even better.

Marc R. Stanley
Stanley Law Group
Former Anchor, KXAS-TV 5 *Faith Focus*

Colleen Brinkmann is the real deal. She lights up a room when she enters, and sincerely engages with everyone she meets. She leads with pure intention, wisdom, transparency and energy. You won't want to miss out on the guidance she shares in this book. If we could all shine like Colleen, the world would be a better place.

Melissa Atkinson
VP, Parkland Foundation, Parkland Health & Hospital System

In a conversational, easy-to-read style, Colleen lays out all the elements required for the success of a monumental fundraising campaign in the nonprofit world. She also highlights and pays homage to the critical non-tactical elements...the emotions, the fears, the spirit and heart that took the campaign to its goal. Inspiring reading!

Aradhana (Anna) Asava
Founding Co-Chair, NTFB Indian-American Council

Inspiring book! A must for anyone interested or engaged in the social entrepreneurial sector. Colleen has laid out the guiding principles for planning, initiating and successfully carrying out a major campaign in the nonprofit sector.

Raj G. Asava
Founding Co-Chair, NTFB Indian-American Council

Colleen's story isn't just about improving your organization. It's about how you can become a better leader with values others will want to follow. Pay close attention.

Jenny Birgé
Corporate and Community Innovator

Colleen and I had a treasured peer relationship pursuing the relentless endeavor to mobilize the public to end hunger. I have the utmost respect and admiration for all she has accomplished both personally and professionally and am honored to have shared a point in time on this journey with her. Her personal stories and insights are an exceptional road map for paid and unpaid leaders seeking to do transformational good in the world.

Dawn Burroughs
VP of Marketing & Communications, Regional Food Bank of
Oklahoma (retired)

This book describes a profoundly important social issue of our times. The situation exists throughout the U.S., so communities nationwide would benefit from this uniquely informative book.

David Bowman
Chairman, TTG Consultants

Having known Colleen for years, I've been aware of and admired her journey tremendously. This is such a clear and helpful message to anyone embarking on a North Star, aspirational goal. Tremendous message on building the team and strategies to accomplish it. It's a generously shared experience that will benefit anyone who has a giant vision and desires guidance on how to accomplish it.

Donna Butterfield
SVP, Frost Bank

This is a book that took a lifetime of experiences to make possible and is worthy of your time to read. Having seen Colleen in action for over fifteen years, the leadership lessons shared in this book seem to have come so easily to her. It is refreshing and inspiring for the rest of us that these lessons can be learned. The leadership journey is different for every traveler. This guide is invaluable for those on the path to improvement.

Lane Cardwell
President, Cardwell Hospitality Advisory
Former Chairman, NTFB Board of Directors

Colleen is one of the most talented and gifted people I know. Her remarkable journey, documented in this book, is informative, insightful and full of solid, transferable principles for anyone wanting to make a difference in the world.

Brad Cecil
President, Brad Cecil & Associates

Colleen Brinkmann spent well over a decade combatting hunger in North Texas with great intellect and passion, as well as the necessary buoyancy to persevere. While the challenge of hunger persists, it's much worse for the wear given Colleen's work—work that has unquestionably laid a great foundation for the fight to continue. One would be hard pressed to find more sage counsel and insight into what is required to achieve success in the nonprofit world than that offered by Colleen.

Justin Chatigny
Executive Director of Marketing, Grant Thornton
Founded NTFB's *Full on Faith* initiative

Colleen Brinkmann is a living legend in relationship-building and effective fundraising. She was amazing to work with and I am so glad she memorialized her recollection of her time at the North Texas Food Bank.

Jeanne Clark, CPA
VP, Finance & Administration, NTFB

Colleen has an energy, authenticity, charm, wit and in-the-moment focus that's very engaging. She is a passionate leader, active listener, effective mentor and undaunted advocate for our neighbors in need. If you have the same zest for learning that Colleen possesses, you will gain insights and skills from this book written by the consummate people-person who is also a strategic, critical thinker and ambitious achiever of challenging goals—especially when the goals to be achieved make our community a better place for all people. I encourage you to read *Moonshot Leadership* today.

Rev. Jay Cole
Executive Director, Crossroads Community Services

Colleen perfectly weaves a blueprint for success for nonprofit leaders who seek to build a transformational brand. As one who recognizes that excellence forges goodness, I think this book is a must-read. Start 2019 right by reading this with your team.

Javiar Collins, NFL Athlete 2001–2007

Colleen Brinkmann is a world-class, purpose-driven leader. Her backstory, sense of purpose and relatable successes and challenges combine to deliver transformative and actionable leadership insights. This book is as practical as it is inspiring!

Lee J. Colan, Ph.D.
Leadership Advisor and Author of *Stick with It*

Colleen authentically shares how vision, leadership, passion and hard work were ignited to tackle life challenges, especially hunger. The learnings from this book can be used to help stop hunger across America. Read it today, to help elevate your leadership and make an impact tomorrow.

Julie Davis-Colan
Co-Founder, The L Group

Fascinating story of fearless leadership, inventive strategy and determined achievement that transformed a nonprofit—the North Texas Food Bank—into a new business model from which many for-profit leaders can learn.

Michael Cox
Former Member, NTFB Board of Directors

Sharing a common heritage and value system with Colleen, I have always keenly observed and admired her strategic and patient leadership. Gabrielle Bernstein once said, if you allow your passion to become your purpose, one day it might just become your profession— and that is the case with Colleen. She has been a compass to many. "Values when crystallized into clear vision, change the world"—and the NTFB team certainly did that! She found a way to leave the valuable legacy of her learnings for other leaders (board members and executive team) and passionate professionals in nonprofit and business. The book encourages readers to align their values with their work, to "let the tea leaves soak" instead of moving too quickly, and the importance of building authentic relationships. It offers numerous opportunities for reflection and pause.

Sejal Desai
Business Engagement Director, Communities Foundation of Texas
Founder, SevaYatra

Clarity, energy, accomplishment—Colleen shares her strengths, learnings and recommendations in this remarkable book which will benefit both nonprofit and business leaders. Speaking from deep experience, she challenges us to hone leadership skills needed for today and for the future.

Fran Eichorst
Vice President, Public Affairs (Retired)

Working on what I like to call "the other side of the house" at NTFB, my fellow Programs and Agencies' colleagues would typically see only the monumental outcomes that resulted from the vision, passion and sheer determination and work of Colleen and her teams over the years. The barriers and struggle to get there were never seen nor heard about. We all know about her ready smile, laugh and interest in everyone with whom she spoke. Reading this book, filled with Colleen's wonderful insights and advice, is one of many things that are inspiring me in my own role as a hunger fighter today. Another is the honor and privilege I feel entering my office each day at the brand-new NTFB Perot Family Campus, looking out of my window over Jan's Garden.

Cynthia Ferris
Director, NTFB Programs and Agencies

Colleen's story is compelling from both a personal and professional standpoint. For nearly two decades I've seen the enormous impact of the North Texas Food Bank through the fearless leadership of Jan Pruitt and Colleen's visionary and strategic abilities, building a brand that raised over $110 million in the past three years. The level of complex strategy and execution required to accomplish this is nearly unheard of in the nonprofit sector. They were truly "the dynamic duo." I encourage business leaders, social entrepreneurs and nonprofit leaders and staff to read this book. You will walk away inspired and equipped with new ways to achieve your own moonshot impact.

Debra Tippett Gibbe
CEO, Cardinal Company
Former Member, NTFB Board of Directors

Truly a divine imprint for the essence of *Moonshot Leadership* in the nonprofit world!

Susan Glen
SVP, Client Relations, CMP

Colleen's book is simultaneously compelling for its candid reflections on her life experiences while providing profound, yet practical, fundraising and self-assessment tools. A valuable read, especially for corporate leaders joining a nonprofit board.

Lois Golbeck, CPA
SVP, Gillham, Golbeck and Associates, Inc. (retired)

I've known Colleen over my 25 years with the Greater Dallas Community of Churches and CitySquare, and she was always driven to perform with excellence. What's important to know is that the driving force behind that was her heart for those on the fringes. This book will be a valuable read for nonprofit executives, especially those in finance and operations, in building a mutual bridge of understanding with the philanthropy team.

Anice Greiner
Comptroller, CitySquare (retired)

Insightful. Engaging. Real. Colleen Brinkman's writing is accessible and entertaining, and a must-read for nonprofit leaders and board members across the sector. She lifts our sights beyond the everyday grind and focuses our energy on big dreams, sharing a toolbox of tricks to navigate the road. *Brava*, Colleen!

Michael G. Guerra
Chief Resource Officer, San Antonio Food Bank

From personal journey to professional triumph, Colleen Brinkmann shines. Her book should be required reading for anyone preparing to undertake their own odds-defying trek.

Andie Hill
NTFB Executive Administrator

Colleen's story is one of deep passion, commitment and authenticity. When combined with her leadership and collaboration insights, her story provides a blueprint for accomplishing the seemingly impossible. Through this story, she has left something of meaning and lasting value for North Texas and the reader for many years to come.

Bill Hogg
Member, NTFB Board of Directors

It is rare to find those special people in life who are a friend, mentor, colleague and boss all in one neon-wrapped package. I wouldn't have the career I do today if it wasn't for Colleen, her wisdom and unrelenting expectations to achieve success, however we define it. She has a unique ability to hold the highest bar of performance while maintaining the freedom and flexibility to make mistakes, learn, and try, try again. If we can all adopt the attitudes and strategies that she shares within these pages, the world will be a much better, less complicated place.

Lauren Banta Holloway
Nonprofit Executive and former NTFB Colleague

The North Texas Food Bank is a model for how to achieve a mission, be compassionate and meet a budget. Colleen Brinkmann was a key member of the leadership team, making big decisions and adding the compassion to the organization. Colleen also knew how and when to recognize donors. As a person responsible for charitable giving, I felt appreciated for the contribution and the results.

Gary Huddleston
Kroger Executive (retired)
Former Member, NTFB Board of Directors

Colleen Brinkmann is the consummate professional in the field of nonprofit development and marketing. Her skill is only outmatched by her warm, pragmatic personality and sincere desire to help other development professionals succeed. What an honor it has been to learn from her!

Teresa Jackson
CEO and Executive Director, Sharing Life Community Outreach

Colleen writes out of an amazing wealth of experience, not as simply a tactician only, but as an artist who spins a compelling story of compassion, tenacity, leadership and, well, just how it is that we can change the world! How fortunate I am to call her friend.

Rev. Larry M. James
CEO, CitySquare

Colleen is a genuine leader who displays great enthusiasm in bringing consensus among diverse sets of ideas and people.   To me, she symbolizes what every young leader should aspire to emulate in their careers.   Her *Char Minar* principles in the book provide the right framework to do just that.

Vijay Jayaraman
Healthcare Executive

This is what great leadership looks like! Colleen shares personal stories and insights from her work in an incredible organization that literally brings abundant life to the world. These are deeply inspiring stories that make for a great study on organizational strategy and execution. Valuable leadership lessons that touch the soul.

Bill Koch
Executive Leadership Coach and former CEO

When I first met Colleen during our Leadership Dallas class, she patiently educated me on the hunger problem in North Dallas and opened my eyes to the dire need not only in the urban areas but the suburbs. She debunked all the myths about hunger while guiding me through the great work of the North Texas Food Bank. This is what good leadership is all about. Her book is a must-read for nonprofit board members, executives and those considering work in the philanthropic field.

Caren Lock
Chair, Dallas Women's Foundation Board of Directors, 2017–2019

Working with Colleen at the Food Bank was an honor. I observed her managing many successful marketing campaigns and leading the fundraising effort to build the new Perot Family Campus. Colleen has built a career dedicated to helping those in need.

Larry Lavine
Turtle Creek Restaurant Group; Founder, Chili's (Brinker)
Former Chairman, NTFB Board of Directors

Colleen's track record at every nonprofit organization she has supported speaks for itself. She left each better off than when she arrived. The lessons she learned during her impressive nonprofit career, chronicled in this book, are applicable to organizations of any size and can be immediately implemented in your own organization. This book illustrates her road map to success and by following her clear steps and tips along the way, you can climb your own Mount Everest with Colleen as your guide!

Victoria Mathews, CFRE
Consultant, Brad Cecil & Associates

Colleen Townsley Brinkmann's book boldly and authentically sets out what it takes to be a leader in the nonprofit world. Colleen weaves her own personal experience into every page and what shines through is her love, compassion and vision for a better world.

Mary Johanna McCurley
Of Counsel, Shackelford, Bowen, McKinley & Norton

Engaging and impactful. Colleen uses her story and the NTFB's journey to provide a helpful leadership guide.

Retta A. Miller
Partner, Jackson Walker LLP
Member, NTFB Board of Directors, 2017 to Present

Colleen Brinkmann has made a significant contribution to the success of the Food Bank. She educated the community through her marketing efforts and expanded the donor network that built the infrastructure to further expand the programs to help people break from the restraints that contribute to chronic hunger and poor nutrition.

Teresa Phillips
Senior Director, ISI
Former Chair, NTFB Board of Directors

Colleen has written a must-read for those looking to drive sustained change in the world through a raw, informative and inspiring look at leadership.

Brian Murphy
SVP, Clear Technologies

Colleen is a dynamic leader and strategic thinker. Her ability to strategize and lead has worked throughout her career no matter where she worked. Her guiding principles are applicable to any organization and at any level.

Barbara Prather
Executive Director, Northeast Iowa Food Bank

This is a thoughtful and inspiring read for both novice fundraisers and seasoned professionals. Heartfelt from the beginning, Colleen captures your attention right away and keeps you engaged as she unfolds her story, along with that of the North Texas Food Bank—about opportunity, lessons learned, the importance of "Here!" and the Food Bank's meteoric rise from grassroots to a locally and nationally recognized nonprofit in hunger relief. Whether you are just starting out or have been in nonprofit for over 25 years, everyone can take one or more pearls of wisdom from this book and apply them to their daily work lives. I know I will. *Brava*, Colleen!

Amy Ragan
Chief Development Officer, Houston Food Bank

For years, people have been asking Colleen about the secrets behind raising so many millions of dollars in such a short period of time. Now, they can find all those priceless lessons in this one book.

Saul Torres
Senior Lead for Creative Direction, AT&T

Colleen brings the rare leadership ability to take on audaciously ambitious goals, mobilize the right team and then win "against all odds." Her humble spirit, a reflection of her heritage from India, is "the shine" which she generously inspires others to own. Whether you are seeking a paid or unpaid position in nonprofit, her insights will set the bar for the type of organization you want to be involved in.

Mahesh Shetty
President & CFO, SG Blocks, Inc.
Chairman, US-India Chamber of Commerce, 2016–2017

As an upper-tier manager for a Fortune 500 company before I retired, and after volunteering for over thirteen years at the North Texas Food Bank, I watched Colleen show how to make a nonprofit organization reach its ultimate potential. Always appreciative of the gift of time, they even named an award after me! Her leadership and knowledge were instrumental in the success of the NTFB.

Mike Snider
Community Leader

I knew Colleen to be articulate and well spoken, but to see the breadth and depth of her knowledge and the way she brought clarity to a complex topic was brilliant. The manner in which she provided a step-by-step explanation of philanthropic approaches went beyond helpful. It was illuminating. What a wonderful gift Colleen has to be able to raise awareness and money for worthy causes. It is even more extraordinary that she is also able to empower others on that path.

Lori A. Spies, PhD, RN, NP-C
Assistant Professor, Baylor University Louise Herrington School of
Nursing

Colleen made me a better parent. She welcomed me and my young children, and their friends and families, to the North Texas Food Bank with open arms, and spoke to my young son Tyler about the hunger problem in Dallas and how it pervaded neighborhoods just a stone's throw away from our own home. She humanized the subject and spoke the kids' language. We have had many conversations around the dinner table since our first visit to NTFB. Thank you, Colleen!

Charmaine A. Tang
Community Volunteer and Business Executive

From the moment I met Colleen during Leadership Dallas in 2015, we connected. Her ability to listen, ask the right questions, share her wisdom, lead others, and most importantly, make things happen, brings success in all that she endeavors. This book is unique because it is written from the heart and the head, and is a must-read for nonprofit leaders, fundraisers and social entrepreneurs. Read it and learn from one of the best.

LuAnn Tarango
Communications, Texas Instruments

I used to believe there were three types of people in this world: those that watch things happen, those that wonder what is happening, and those that make things happen. After having the great fortune of working with Colleen, and also becoming friends, I have added a fourth type: those that make things happen that better our world.

Robert Walters
VP, AT&T

Before you start your capital campaign or your next big nonprofit adventure, read this book! Colleen Brinkmann has always been one of our nation's best fundraising and communication professionals, and one of my personal heroes. I am thrilled that she has taken the time to share her experience and her learning with the rest of us through this book. Thank you, Colleen, for your inspiration and the good that is sure to come from you sharing your magic!

Kristin Warzocha
President and CEO, Greater Cleveland Food Bank

Often the difference between motivating someone to do their best and inspiring them to greatness is how you make them feel. Colleen has illustrated this ability through inspiring vast strength, conjured from depths unknown, to achieve seemingly impossible results. She applies this forte with an adept subtlety that is cleverly revealed in this book. It could take a lifetime to learn it on your own, or you could have the honor of working alongside Colleen, as I did. This book takes you on a journey of turning astounding feats into reality, while making the process appear straightforward and easy.

Cynthia Wenban
Director of Quality Engineering, Lockheed Martin Corporation(retired)

Former Member, NTFB Board of Directors

RSW has worked with Colleen for over twelve years. I've gotten to know her as a uniquely smart and dedicated leader with a keen perspective and understanding of marketing, development, teamwork and the nonprofit world. More importantly, I've seen her passion in working to create a hunger-free, healthy North Texas—all elements that have led to countless successful activations for North Texas Food Bank and have contributed to closing the hunger gap.

Brad Wines
President, RSW Creative

One of the first people I met when I joined the North Texas Food Bank as a board member was Colleen Brinkmann. From that very first day in 2008 I knew I could count on her sunny view of the world to brighten my day and my perspective. Colleen and Jan Pruitt were a very dynamic team who seemingly always knew where they wanted to be. This book tells the story of their relationship and teamwork in a way that made me reflect on the meetings and opportunities I had to listen to them explain the North Texas Food Bank story. That story constantly evolved over time as the community pushed the Food Bank leaders to provide more to help prevent hunger. These two leaders met the challenge in their years of working together, and I hope the Dallas community can help the Food Bank continue to evolve to new challenges over the next twenty years.

Jon Wolkenstein
Partner, Grant Thornton LLP
Former Chairman, NTFB Board of Directors

Colleen's efforts at the North Texas Food Bank enabled the phenomenal growth that we experienced during her years of service. She brought an understanding of the importance of developing relationships at all levels and applied it across the board, from first-time volunteers to major donors. Her ability to "tell the story" of the organization effectively and get others to do the same contributed significantly to her success. This story of her time at the North Texas Food Bank is a fascinating and compelling read that will help others understand some of the key elements of successful fundraising in the nonprofit arena.

Paul Wunderlich
Former COO, NTFB

With her captivating storytelling, Colleen motivates readers to both reflect and anticipate the bold possibilities for the future.

Erica Yaeger
Chief External Affairs Officer, NTFB

Moonshot Leadership: Catalyzing an Enduring Nonprofit Brand (Against All Odds)

Cover photography from Rachel DeLira

Book jacket designed by Kim Iltis

Design support by RSW Creative

Moonshot Leadership

Catalyzing an Enduring Nonprofit Brand

(Against All Odds)

Colleen Townsley Brinkmann

Powered by CMP

Edited by Joe Frodsham and Maryanne Piña-Frodsham

Dedication

To my parents, Eileen Betty Hakim Townsley and Dr. Rev. Hendrix A. Townsley, who prepared me for this journey even before I realized it; to Barney who continually nourishes my pursuits and neon dreams; and to Rob, Jessica, and Dylan, my brilliant lights.

In Memory of

Jan Pruitt, the ultimate moonshot leader.

Your purchase of *Moonshot Leadership* supports the critical work of the:

Atlanta Community Food Bank
Chicago Food Depository
North Texas Food Bank

Table of Contents

Preface

As I'll share soon, I was bone-weary but also feeling bathed in holy waters of gratitude. I was leaving my "work home" after sixteen years with the North Texas Food Bank and had received generous salutes and farewells. In the prior months, as we slogged away together to complete this historic capital campaign, I'd find myself thinking that our efforts were a real case study of how to reach the moon against all odds.

For over three decades, I worked alongside local and national nonprofits, battling in the trenches with peer fundraisers, marketers and CEOs. I knew with certainty that what we had achieved at the Food Bank could be applied to other organizations across the nation. Our limits had been tested in the past three years, and we were resilient enough to survive and thrive.

After a few weeks of savoring the sweetness of silence at home, I decided to share my story. I spent three days pouring over my new laptop with index cards and sticky notes, and the occasional paper towel filled with Sharpie notes as words rushed from my brain in a tumbled stream of consciousness. I had to dig deep and find the truth about my good and tough times.

One thing I knew for certain: The volcanic spark that creates innovation and transformation comes together when a smart, engaged board hires an authentic, fearless leader who leads with compassion.

Jan Pruitt, the Food Bank's recently deceased CEO, was just that type of leader. She always operated from her core belief that all people deserve a place at America's table.

If a few of these words stir your heart, give you fuel to challenge the status quo or step up into your own moonshot journey, then the world is better for it.

You have not finished your journey. There is more that awaits your impact.

Of that I am certain.

Twenty years from now you will be more disappointed by the things you didn't do than by the ones you did do, so throw off the bowlines, sail away from safe harbor, catch the trade winds in your sails. Explore. Dream. Discover.

– Mark Twain

Introduction

On Friday afternoon, January 28, 2018, I exhaled—profoundly and from my toes. My "Third Season," a moniker I coined for "retirement," was beginning.

We had just secured the final gifts that would propel the North Texas Food Bank's three-year, $55 million capital campaign, *Stop Hunger Build Hope,* over the finish line. Equally eye-popping was the fact that when combined with what was raised for annual operations with the $55 million, the Food Bank had secured over **$110 million** in three years in the face of immense challenges.

Over the past sixteen years, I had led a rigorous focus on building an enduring brand and infusing a mind-set of excellent customer service, and with my award-winning team it had paid off. The North Texas Food Bank (NTFB) was seen everywhere with neon vibrancy and integrity. Paid and unpaid media, grassroots campaigns and a recent market study ranked NTFB No. 1 in unaided brand awareness. Database records had grown from seven thousand to nearly five hundred thousand, and public support had increased 588 percent since I'd joined NTFB in 2002 to lead their marketing, communications, volunteer and, eventually, fundraising efforts. North Texans' response had been loud and explicit. Hunger was unacceptable.

I was exhausted yet deeply fulfilled.

I had just passed the baton to Erica Yaeger, a talented, newly hired executive. Awaiting me was a fresh new canvas on which I could place whatever color I wanted. Or not. It was my choice. Pinch me.

The 82,000-square-foot North Texas Food Bank food distribution facility and offices were quiet. Most staff had left after the post-holiday party and I was able to quietly stroll through familiar spaces inside and out, easily slipping back in time.

There was a serendipitous feel to this wintery, late January afternoon. I had fallen in love with the Food Bank's mission during a warehouse tour conducted by then-COO Paul Wunderlich nearly sixteen years before to the day and time. Now as I made my exit, the same winter sun was warming my face and heart.

Expressions of love and thanks from my team, newly hired CEO Trisha Cunningham, the NTFB Board of Directors, colleagues and friends had bathed me in what I call sacred water. Collectively, a mighty team of paid and unpaid champions over the past three years had achieved the historic $55 million capital campaign while also raising an additional $17–$18 million

Jan Pruitt, NTFB CEO (1999-2016)

Trisha Cunningham, NTFB CEO (2017-Present)

annually for operations despite never-ending, gut-wrenching obstacles. Typically, campaigns of this size occur within academic, healthcare or art circles, not social service organizations. That said, if any organization was poised to tackle this, it was the North Texas Food Bank. Longtime former CEO Jan Pruitt had built a powerhouse of an organization in her twenty years, and Trisha was now going to take it to the next level.

The North Texas Food Bank: From 1982 to Now

NTFB was created around Kathy Hall's kitchen table in 1982 when four courageous food industry leaders—Jo Curtis, Lorraine Griffin Kircher, Liz Minyard and Kathy—thought that unsaleable retail food could benefit those facing hunger. With the gift of the distribution center by Bette Perot (of the Perot Family Foundation), the organization was now in business. By the end of its first year, four hundred thousand pounds of food were distributed to regional pantries, soup kitchens and shelters, based in no small measure on donations of food and expertise from Minyard, Kroger, Tom Thumb and food wholesalers. Area nonprofits now had a steady food supplier. Similarly, across the nation a network of food banks was being formed, leading to the creation of a national association now called Feeding America.

I joined NTFB in February 2002, Jan Pruitt's third year. She had just finished building her team and realigning the organizational chart. Her next goal was to build the brand, a message she had clearly received from the board of directors. The public was contributing just over $2 million and 25,000 volunteer hours annually, which supported the distribution of 20,000 pounds of food. The staff team of forty was scrappy, grassroots and on a first-name basis. Jan believed all things were possible and was able to attract likeminded paid and volunteer talent to the mission. We were building something significant and felt empowered. It was a great place to work.

Little did we imagine that the hunger issue in North Texas would grow so immense that by 2017 the Food Bank would be distributing 190,000 nutritious meals *daily* while the need was even greater.

So Why This Book?

The NTFB story is the culmination of the many lessons I've learned over my thirty years of supporting growth and change in transformational organizations. Some of the lessons were hard-earned through mistakes and lost opportunities. Others came from crucial mentors and some successes along the way. This book intends to provide a "wet cement" blueprint for leaders, paid and volunteer, of other purpose-driven organizations who have a mandate for transformational change and a stretch vision. It also aims to stir the heart. I hope these learnings and stories offer insight, clarification and affirmation to fuel your work to make good happen.

The Food Bank growth story is illustrative of three universal requirements of transformational change:

1) Visionary, bold leadership
2) A culture of innovation (without fear of punishment)
3) The rigor of brand building

These requirements are especially critical in times of growth and change. In fact, growth and change within communities, families and organizations require leadership. And when the objective is longer term and a little outrageous, it requires what I call "Moonshot Leadership." Like President Kennedy's public commitment to put a human on the moon before the end of the 1960s, the NTFB Moonshot was to solve hunger in an area larger and more populous than many countries. Although hunger remains an issue across our nation, NTFB has developed a ten-year strategic program and scale to close the hunger gap. This Moonshot Leadership was enabled by an authentic and enduring brand that is bigger than me, and even our former Food Bank leader, Jan.

Childhood place of magic: 4 Battery Lane, Old Delhi, India

7

4 Battery Lane

As with any story, there is a beginning. Mine started in Old Delhi, India, where I was often happiest exploring the thick, damp emerald-green jungle behind our hundred-year-old brown stone bungalow on Battery Lane, climbing banana trees and playing with neighborhood friends. My upbringing, the values I was taught and the broad worldview my parents instilled in me served as my compass.

If my parents were alive today, they would each be 106. My mother, Eileen Betty Hakim, was a highly accomplished Indian educator who, by the age of 35, had been pegged to lead Isabella Thoburn College in Lucknow. She was akin to the "Golda Meir" of India—fiery, driven but compassionate, and confident that education was the key to justice and peace. Her mother, one of India's early Methodist women physicians, died at the age of 42 having contracted the plague from a patient during a home visit. Eileen was 12, far away in boarding school, and forever mourned her loss.

My dad was a vivacious, blonde-haired, blue-eyed California preacher's kid who, armed with a mechanical engineering degree from UC Berkeley, sailed under the Golden Gate Bridge on a rugged Japanese freighter to serve as a Methodist missionary in India. It was 1936, Hendrix Atkinson Townsley was 24, and India was in a juggernaut fight with Britain for her independence. Within the next few years, he learned four native languages and was more comfortable in Indian garb and turbans than the Western clothing he'd grown up in. I thought of him as the "Lawrence of Arabia" of India. Posted in South Indian villages, he built schools and hospitals, and after fifteen years was appointed to a new regional leadership role in the capital city of New Delhi. Hendrix easily made friends, from villagers to the Nizam of Hyderabad, who later would loan his summer lake palace for Hendrix's honeymoon in Jaipur.

My parents met at a conference, after which they secretly exchanged three hundred love letters over eight months, since many Indians and Westerners disapproved of mixed-race marriages. "Your children will be spotted," wrote one American church leader to my father. Despite these pressures, they married. My sister K (Kay) and I are grateful. Their love flowed from a deep reservoir of shared vision, mutual respect and a fierce desire to create a more just world. Fiery dinnertime debates on political and religious issues of the day were commonplace, evoking a plea for a truce from either K or me.

I realize that these two words—justice and compassion— were embedded into our DNA from the minute K and I were born. We were as comfortable in leper colonies and villages as we were during visits with India's prime ministers and presidents. By the time I was 16, our parents had shown us thirty-two countries on a shoestring budget. We traveled by Cunard ocean liners, cars and trains to Egypt, the Fiji Islands, Australia and New Zealand, the U.S., Europe and through the Panama Canal locks.

After graduating from the American International School in New Delhi in 1971, I left for the University of the Pacific (UOP) in

Stockton, California. Preparations for American college life were underway for weeks. An elderly Indian tailor would stitch Sears-patterned dresses and bell-bottom pantsuits for me while crouched on the bungalow veranda, navigating my mother's treasured Singer sewing machine. Little did I know at that time that I'd quickly discard his pastel-flower creations for the mass-produced, generic velour fashions found in California's big-box stores.

After two years at UOP, I transferred to Southern Methodist University (SMU) in Dallas, Texas, where my parents had retired. Eighteen months later I earned a BFA degree in studio art, began working at local design firms, married SMU classmate Gordon Hager in 1978, and settled down in a Dallas suburb. Our son Rob and daughter Jessica soon followed. Then, my world shifted—hard. In 1986, my father was diagnosed with stage 4 leukemia and died within six weeks. Four months later, my mother was diagnosed with breast cancer and passed away two years after. The loss of my parents was massive and sucked the air out of my life.

I was 35 at the time of the second funeral, had just finished work on a thirty-part educational television series set to air on PBS, and was working full-time at Eastfield College managing ninety adjunct faculty members. My husband and I had a routine of dinner at 6 p.m. before he left for his overnight shift in law enforcement. Home and work were in balance—except for the cavernous hole left by my parents' deaths.

In the days following my mother's funeral, I would find myself sitting in my campus office staring out the window thinking, "I want to do something meaningful in my life so when I die I know I've made an impact." Over and over, day after day, I'd hear that message. I didn't know exactly what "meaningfulness" looked like, but I was determined to find out.

The best way to find yourself is to lose yourself in the service to others.

– Mahatma Gandhi

Dad always felt at home in India, 1937

Mom driving Red Rocket in South India, 1945

My parents' wedding in Bareilly, India, 1945

L.A. to Bombay, a 30-day journey by ship, 1959

Settling into college life in California

Graduation day with my mom, 1971

Our family of four, 1959

13

"Here!"

It took me eighteen months to
unpack what "meaningfulness"
meant. My already-bulging
Rolodex began to expand as I
made new connections within
the community. I was seeking
that moment when my inner
voice would scream, "Here! This
is where you need to be." I was a
young, creative, connect-the-
dots problem-solver and project
manager. My worldview was

Rev. Tom Quigley, mentor and friend

global, and not limited to one faith or set of cultural norms. After
all, my home in Old Delhi was often called "Grand Central Station"
because of the continuous flow of diverse visitors—Buddhist
monks, village preachers, American bishops, Sikh and Jain
businessmen, and beatnik American relatives.

That loud "Here!" occurred when Tom Quigley, director of
the Greater Dallas Community of Churches, offered me the dual
roles of director of communications and producer of KXAS' *Faith
Focus* weekly television program. The show had been on the blocks
for months while the producer/host faced legal challenges. Soon,
Tom would become one of my most important mentors who
modeled social justice and taught me to write. He gave me a wide

berth from which to build, fail and restart. For eight years I was in Shangri-La.

One month into my new job, I looked at my first paycheck and thought, "I cannot believe I get paid to do what I just did." I felt the same way for the next thirty years.

Tom was inspiring, authentic and supportive of my drive to transform a show that had dismal sub-zero Nielsen ratings into a local powerhouse. The thirty-minute time slot was waiting for thought-provoking content on faith and ethics, ready to be reinvented. The number of sponsors grew from the initial four to fourteen, representing a diverse array of faith traditions. Auditions were now held from which I'd select on-air talent, adding film and music critics and preproduced packages on stories best told from the community instead of the studio. When the fifteenth anniversary show garnered higher ratings than the Daytona 500, station manager Brian Hocker was shocked. "I can't believe this," he said. "Locally, more people are watching the *Faith Focus* anniversary show than the race." The trust and freedom Tom had provided me allowed me to create a thought-provoking, thirty-minute weekly experience on faith and ethics. I was singing.

Money has never been the driving force in my search for meaning. That said, my husband and I always knew we needed to be a two-income household. My point here is that while we were a two-income household, the monetary gain was not the work out if I was in the right place. That belief has borne itself out over these thirty years.

After eight years with GDCC, Tom departed for a position in Seattle, a new director arrived, and I found myself unmoored. I needed to see a place where I could, once again, hear the clarion cry of my inner voice.

Then, I got The Call.

Thriving in Chaos Without Knowing the Language

"Hi, I'm Carol Childress with Leadership Network, and I was referred to you by Sharon Grigsby of *The Dallas Morning News.* I want to talk with you about a job." Her staccato, direct tone indicated she was not open to debate. We talked.

Within a month, I joined this private foundation created and funded by Bob Buford and his mentor, Peter Drucker. I was the fourteenth employee when I arrived, and when I left nearly five years later, there were forty-five. I jumped into this think tank with both feet and found the learning curve steep but enticing. I was not familiar with the growing evangelical church movement of large congregations led by charismatic Hawaiian-shirted pastors. Carol quickly took me under her wing, taking me on a flurry of church visits across the country and bringing me to interviews with senior pastors, radical theologians and change agents. My head was spinning. These churches were definitely not my "grandmother's church." And certainly not what I had grown up with in India.

Titles, steeples, denominational monikers, robes (both pastoral and choir) and familiar worship format were gone. In their place was more of an experience, defined as "authentic" and "real world," which was drawing thousands of churched and unchurched to learn about capital-G God. Workplace discussions were often passionate, fast-paced, intellectual, competitive and inspiring. It was as if I was in a foreign land without knowing the language but was expected to converse fluently. It was not a comfortable feeling. Nevertheless, it was precisely within this environment that I gained the insights and new abilities which directly helped my work building the NTFB brand and customer service culture later on. I pushed myself to spend days with innovators and thought leaders across the country, interviewing them about the "why"—why are you reinventing the religious experience, and for what outcomes? I was hungry for answers and would come back loaded with insights that I shared with the executive team. On one occasion I remember having the courage to tell this team that a specific well-known older pastor had told me that our organization was now passé—irrelevant to his ministry because we had not come up with any new innovations. While that was hard to hear, it was that type of brave candor that made Leadership Network the leading think tank for the large church movement in those days.

Personal Application #1

Where have you found yourself in a foreign land without knowing the language? Reflect on what you were pushed, propelled or forced to learn during that season, and how those learnings have helped you be successful today. Alternatively, have you always been in a safe space yet are yearning to stretch? If so, what are some steps you can take to explore enticing new ground that can propel you to fresh ways?

My Exclamation Point

I worked with, and for, the "Steve Jobs" of nonprofit. That's what I sometimes called Jan Pruitt, who hired me over a rushed lunch of Chinese food in February of 2002. We first met when I was producing *Faith Focus*, but in the ensuing years our paths had gone in different directions. Now, my resume had made its way to her at the Food Bank.

"So, what have you been doing?" she asked. I bubbled forth with stories from Leadership Network and how I was seeking opportunities to impact core human needs on a large scale. Her bright blue eyes peered intently at my face as she asked a few probing questions. In the end, she told me to call the director of operations, Paul Wunderlich. "He gives the best tours of our food distribution operations," she said. "Then, call me." Within twenty-four hours I had scheduled a tour with Paul for the following week.

It was a beautiful, crisp, late January afternoon when I pulled into the Food Bank parking lot. I almost drove past the large beige warehouse because the brown wooden sign was weather worn and in need of paint. The parking lot was nearly empty as it was close to the end of the workday. Paul warmly welcomed me as I stepped into the small, softly cluttered and worn beige-walled lobby. Torn old magazines and a vase with dusty plastic flowers covered the small table flanked by folding chairs that had seen better days. Slightly faded nature photographs, the kind you see in low-budget motels, hung on the walls. "Let's go this way," he gestured as we went through the employee breakroom, which still had the lingering scent of slightly burnt coffee residue and microwaved lunches. Through a door that had an ironic sign "No Food or Drink Allowed," we stepped into the dimly lit warehouse filled with racks of shrink-wrapped food stacked thirty feet high.

Up and down the aisles we walked as Paul shared how the food industry, farmers and the public donated unsaleable products that volunteers would repackage so hundreds of regional charities could then feed their hungry clients. The only sound other than Paul's voice was the constant soft buzz of the fluorescent lighting and freezers. Stepping over sheetrock debris, he pointed out that in a few months a 3,000-square-foot production kitchen would be ready to provide up to ten thousand precooked, frozen casseroles weekly, a new concept few food banks were considering at that time.

Paul stopped in front of a massive steel door to a drive-through freezer. I'd never seen anything like it. The afternoon winter sunlight was streaming through a murky skylight thirty feet up as facts and figures about supply chain, freezers, trucks and health codes spilled forth. In that very moment, I knew the issue of hunger was for me. I had found it.

I realized that the sheer scale of what they were doing every day was like the space shuttle's rocket boosters kicking in to thrust the ship out of the gravitational pull of Earth—it was absolutely crucial, if seemingly impossible.

I thanked Paul and walked to my car. The parking lot was now empty except for my cute red Mazda Miata convertible. I started up the engine, threw down the top and zoomed out of the parking lot and down the road to the interstate. The sun was warming my face. I could feel my chubby cheeks pushing up against my sunglasses.

I was smiling.

The next morning, I called Jan. "I want to come work there," I told her.

Now, at this point, she had not offered me a job or even indicated there was an appropriate opening. She asked me what my salary was and I told her. I could hear her flipping over what sounded like large ledger sheet pages. "Well, I don't have that much in the budget, but I can offer you this." I immediately accepted her figure, knowing everything else would work itself out. And it did.

Thus, began my Exclamation Point season of life.

Chapter 1

The Genesis: Your Leadership Fuels the Purpose

Great happens from the inside out. But first, you must know yourself.

At the heart of every organizational change and advancement is leadership. People who operate against the conventional wisdom or beliefs of the day take a leap of faith and drive toward an idea or ideal. This is true of any advancement—from Susan B. Anthony to Bill Gates, to the myriad of lesser-known people you have seen lead in different aspects of your life. These transformational leaders come from all backgrounds and styles. However, what is similar is an internal conviction to a set of values. Values, when crystallized into a clear vision, change the world.

I genuinely believe values are a combination of choice and circumstance, often shaped in our formative years and reinforced through decisions and experiences as we move through life. Aligning your values with your work is the source of personal meaning and impact.

This is why leadership starts with knowing yourself. Specifically, your values. I began this book by sharing the genesis of my values by telling my story. It provided context for the fundamental principles in succeeding chapters. Most importantly, I hope it prompts you to think of your own story and values. To support your reflections, I have included select exercises throughout the book. I encourage you to take the time to complete these exercises and consider how they can be applied to your work.

Every organization's culture and brand start with values-driven leadership. Moreover, leaders must know the source of their values. My values, honed while growing up in India and sharpened due to the untimely deaths of my parents, shaped my worldview and leadership style.

My Four Core Values:

1. Respect

In India I witnessed my parents treating people of all walks of life equally— gently holding the gnarled hand of a leper while intently listening to his story or debating divergent views on religious freedom with Prime Minister Indira

Centenary Methodist Church, New Delhi, India

Gandhi. I had a front row seat to what respect looked like. When my mechanical engineer father built a new Methodist church in New Delhi, he designed into the logo and architecture the scalloped motif found in all Mughal structures. He fervently believed that to build true community one must respect the culture you are stepping into. To this day, Centenary Methodist Church has this design, with both Muslim and Hindu elements, in its logo, pews and altar. This belief has continued to be a powerful guide for me.

Under Jan's leadership, NTFB set ambitious annual goals that her executive team was accountable for achieving. To be successful everyone had to operate in full-throttle mode and be strong and adaptable to rapid change. The high standards of performance I held for myself and others, especially during the formative high-growth years, crystallized who was wired for the culture and who would soon leave. Lauren Banta Holloway, a high performer who, during her six years with NTFB, held various positions, each with increased responsibilities, valued the high expectations. She says they gave her "the freedom and flexibility to make mistakes, learn and try, try again."

It took hiring a VP-level in HR to build the appropriate strength needed to achieve the ambitious annual growth goals. This helped create a stronger team culture built on mutual respect and collaboration.

I instilled an open door policy, and we held team meetings that were a safe place to share failures and ideas. We celebrated individual and group achievements in timely and meaningful ways, and offered diverse approaches to grow professionally. As our work became more complex, requiring strategy and analysis, I'd tell a frustrated team member to talk to me when they were stuck, and I'd help them remove the roadblock. Because of my own wiring and years of navigating NTFB, I felt good helping someone find an open pathway to their success.

Friend- and fund-raising is both an art and science. Principles, strategies, techniques and tactics are the science. These can be taught and calibrated based on cultural and demographic shifts. The art? Well, it certainly can be taught, but to be *really good* at it one must have the elements in your DNA, heart and soul. However, without a culture of respect, it doesn't matter how much "art" and "science" you have within your team.

Nothing was more important at NTFB than retaining the brand and trust of the public. Soon after joining NTFB, I noticed that the fundraising team was about to sell our donor database to a local nonprofit. It hit me like a gut punch. I immediately finalized a privacy policy that informed donors and the public that we do not share, rent or sell their information, and embedded it into all of our communication channels and collateral. While this may seem like an obvious decision today, realize that in 2002 there wasn't a vociferous mind-set about data security like we have today.

2. Excellence

Generally, there is a different (and lower) set of expectations for nonprofits than the for-profit world. That's because nonprofit organizations, as well-meaning as they may be, don't have the plethora of resources found in for-profit businesses. But that's never been the measuring stick for setting my operating standards. Why can't we strive to be as smart, strategic, clear and polished as anyone in a for-profit environment? When I was a team of one at the Food Bank, I made sure my thinking, actions, communications and preparations were the best they could be. As the team grew, I instilled the importance of research, strategic thinking, preparation and customer service. It was satisfying to sit quietly in any number of key donor meetings and watch NTFB professionals artfully claim the moment by efficiently presenting a polished case for support. Rarely did they walk away with a "no." By embedding a culture of excellence vertically and horizontally, the level of trust and respect we gained grew. It also attracted a larger talent pool of fundraisers and marketers equipped for the NTFB challenge.

3. Transparency

It's vital that transparency be a part of the oxygen you breathe as a leader and team member. Having the self-confidence to be transparent internally and externally fosters goodwill and trust, both priceless. After all, ensuring your brand remains valued is second to none, and transparency plays a key role in achieving this. Be open to sharing your failures and missteps and how they served as learning moments for you. Convey them in a timely and succinct manner, organically—as it fits the moment. I've had to apologize to team members, donors and on a few occasions some in the public who disagreed with issues of hunger relief. No one is perfect or knows all. It truly is better to step forward and address the matter in a timely, open and honest manner.

During the capital campaign's final year, my whiteboard was continually being updated with prospects, projected gift amounts and notes. Every few days, a name would be removed, calibrated or added. It was my ground zero. Every few days I'd huddle with one or more members of my team to discuss progress. On some days, gifts I was responsible for securing did not materialize. No matter how hard I had worked it, the stars were just not aligned. While I was disappointed, there was too much to do to waste time on regrets. I found it easiest to give my team the update, explain why and move forward with the remaining prospects. I'd often remind fundraisers that we were not the IRS and couldn't *make* someone give us a gift. Our organization's financials were viewable on our website, and I was known for allowing TV crews to shoot B-roll footage of our warehouse without my constant oversight. While I knew most of the media, I also knew that by allowing them some unsupervised access it would clearly convey that the North Texas Food Bank had nothing to hide. That message was priceless and the strategy never failed.

4. Fun

Creating an internal team environment of organic and planned fun does not cost a lot. But it generates priceless value exemplified in team retention, productivity and effectiveness. While we were increasingly a hard-driving team, we focused on hiring for fit and teaching the rest. Workspaces reflected each team member's life and style; impromptu coffee runs and celebrations for big and small achievements were held (and initiated by anyone on the team). Receiving a full or half day of PTO as a surprise "thank you" was one of the most popular ways to be saluted. Along with celebrating birthdays, births and hiring anniversaries, one team might host a themed recognition for another department that had just completed a significant project, with surprises left on each desk. For years, the fundraising team would host an early morning Appreciation Breakfast for the NTFB truck drivers and operations team, as they were our key ambassadors, interfacing with bulk food donors and volunteers on a daily basis. Their service directly impacted public support of the organization. Ownership of this core value resided with everyone in philanthropy. Food bankers across the country would often talk about the invisible wall between external-facing teams and operations/programs.

Each area of business would often feel like the other side did not understand the urgency of their work. To break down these barriers at NTFB, we infused big and little efforts to bring different departments together or the whole team. When Jan's annual work anniversary or birthday would approach, we'd produce an all-staff video or a massive butcher-paper poster that everyone signed. When operations earned a Feeding America award, the fundraising and marketing teams surprised them with an impromptu party. Once a year, Jan would invite a diverse array of staff to drop by a board meeting to get acquainted.

The above four core values were embedded into our annual fundraising and marketing plans with strategies and measurable outcomes for each one. If we were to achieve transformational

27

heights as an organization, it was non-negotiable: we had to strive to live and breathe these values every day.

Feet, what do I need you for when I have wings to fly?

– Frida Kahlo

NTFB's fearless philanthropy and operations teams, 2017

Personal Application #2

Before we get further along, take a few minutes to reflect on your core values and those of your organization. How do your core values align (or not) with where you are planted today? When picturing the ideal organization where you can shine, what would be its guiding principles?

My NTFB Story is Not about Magic

It is a flesh and blood tale of how a remarkable team stepped up at critical, oxygen-escaping-the-room moments to say, "Hunger is unacceptable." The makeup of my team would ebb and flow over time, along with the level of commitment and skill, yet fundraising results were exceptional.

How can that be?

In my early years at the Food Bank, I found the external soil receptive to fresh ideas for raising awareness and engaging individuals and families, businesses, the food industry, media, elected leaders, corporate executives, and the faith, civic and academic communities. Some years later, I realized that this powerful momentum of public support carried us forward even though internally our executive and external-facing teams lacked cohesiveness.

I had planned to retire in 2015; however, Jan asked me to stay to lead the three-year capital campaign (2015–2018) and then retire afterward. As anyone who knew Jan can attest, it was hard to say no to her. I also realized she was offering me a once-in-a-lifetime capstone experience from which to sail away.

Little did I know what gut-wrenching challenges lay ahead.

Four months into the capital campaign in August 2015, Jan was diagnosed with cancer. She juggled aggressive treatment schedules while continuing to lead the organization and help with the capital campaign. By the following June, my husband was diagnosed with lung cancer and had emergency surgery to remove a malignancy in his upper right lobe. A month later, Jan went on medical leave. COO Simon Powell stepped in as interim CEO, bringing much-needed stability.

There were weeks when I felt like I was driving a stagecoach led by wild horses who were unable to avoid the flood of boulders and rocks on an unpaved road.

Jan passed away January 3, 2017, after a fierce eighteen-month battle. It was also the beginning of our third and final year of the capital campaign. The preparation that comes with a critical illness did not lessen the deep sadness and feeling of uncertainty that prevailed among the Food Bank staff and core supporters.

What kept the campaign moving forward in those final months was a remarkable resilience and sense of care between the executive team, staff at all levels, campaign co-chairs, the board and the campaign committee. This cohesiveness multiplied in the final six months once CEO Trisha Cunningham came on board. She hit the ground running, nailing the last $4 million to close the campaign on schedule.

Moonshot Learnings: You Need to Choose a New Animal to Be
Kate Maehr, CEO, Chicago Food Depository

Let me start by saying that Jan Pruitt taught me a lot. I mean A LOT. I feel like she plucked me out of nowhere and encouraged me to get involved in our national network. I learned how committees should operate and meetings should run, saw how coalitions are built and consensus achieved. From the State Association Task Force (chaired by Jan—I was invited to join when I had been CEO of the Food Depository for a whopping six months), to Feeding America's National Council (NAC), to the Feeding America CEO search committee, to the Feeding America Board of Directors—she led me, she taught me, and she inspired me.

The greatest lessons I learned from Jan weren't about consensus, but instead were about conflict. As you know, part of Jan's real genius was to see people. She was quick to size up a person's strengths, but also their vulnerabilities. In my case, from almost our first meeting she knew that I was conflict averse. I was the one at meetings who usually piped in with, "Well, I can see both sides..." Jan probably understood what a challenge this might be for me as a new and relatively young CEO. I can still remember her taking me aside during a break at a State Association Task Force meeting and asking, "What do you think?" As I stammered, she simply said, "You need to think about why you are here—and it's not to agree with everything else that's been said." It felt like a blow to the stomach. And yet, there was something in Jan that made you want to live up to the high bar she set. So, I went back into those meetings, and I learned as I watched her. One of my favorite moments—and this happened often—came when she would say, "I can say this because Kate knows I love her..." and then proceed to disagree with me on something I had just said.

During those meetings, and so many meetings after, I learned that you could state your opinion, disagree—even conflict—and that's okay. While I never mastered the Texas twang and didn't have sparkling blue eyes, I learned you could disagree with grace, warmth and love.

Moonshot Learnings: You Need to Choose a New Animal to Be
Kate Maehr, CEO, Chicago Food Depository (Contd.)

I took those many lessons about conflict and the art of disagreeing back with me into my food bank. Over the years, Jan counseled me many times before I mustered the courage to assert a different view with staff, board and donors. The lessons applied outside of work—in my relationships with my husband and sons, my parents, brothers and friends. Being brave and saying what I believed to be true, even when it was hard and unpopular, became a part of myself I was able to claim thanks to Jan.

Not long before she got sick, Jan and I were joking about my conflict adversity. I laughed and said, "You know, when you get right down to it, I'm a golden retriever. I want to be loved by everyone." She didn't laugh back, but instead she put her hands on my shoulders and said, "You know what, Kate? You need to choose a new animal to be."

In the three years since that conversation, I've confronted more challenges—and more conflicts—than I ever dreamed possible. So, at each turn, I've tried to remember that I get to choose the animal I want to be. Moreover, I've tried to remember why I'm at the table. Those two lessons from Jan have guided me well. I have a feeling Jan may be watching over me. If that's true, she's seen the way I've maneuvered these challenges. I've probably done some things differently than she would have. If that's the case, I hope she's leaning over to the next person in heaven saying, "You know, I can say this because Kate knows I love her..."

www.ChicagosFoodBank.org

Chapter 2
The NTFB Story: Principles of Growth Learned Along the Way

Authentic leadership creates the right culture in which innovations foster transformational impact.

Of this I am certain. I lived it.

"You have three things to do," Jan said as I started my new job as director of communications in February of 2002. "The newsletter, media and our website." I was a team of one. Chris Culak was director of development, tasked with raising more than $2 million annually to support the distribution of 20 million meals. NTFB was the food supplier for more than 150 North Texas nonprofit pantries, afterschool programs, shelters, soup kitchens and senior centers. A large push-pin map, which cost us $200 (an exorbitant sum for us at the time), showed each location. I was grateful that a corporate donor agreed to cover the cost of the map. That was my first fundraising success.

A year later, Chris left and a new director of development, Elizabeth Averill, was hired. My longtime marriage had ended and I was learning to navigate unfamiliar terrain. My responsibilities at work expanded to include brand building, marketing, direct mail, events and campaigns. "I was hired to build the brand, and the board of directors has said success is when *The Dallas Morning News* runs our story on page one of Metro, above the fold and with a color photo," Jan explained. Five years later, NTFB board member and KPMG executive Steve Chase brought a large group of associates to volunteer on Hunger Action Day, an annual, nationally recognized day in September. Having already learned a disciplined approach to cultivating relationships in newsrooms with editorial boards and industry trade publications, I pitched the story of KPMG volunteering. The next day, orange-shirted KPMG associates were featured in an article and photo above the fold and on the front page of Metro.

There was little in place in the areas of marketing, communications, volunteer experience and brand building when I joined NTFB, so the ground was fertile. The public's financial support came from a modest direct mail program, major gifts from foundations and individuals, and handling fees agencies would pay for food. It was not a robust pipeline, had a dangerous dependence on a few major donors, and wasn't tapping into the vast and expanding North Texas marketplace. I needed to ignite the public behind Jan's vision and the mission, and I needed a team. Starting with two marketing and event staff members and one volunteer coordinator, I began shaping the team using a marketing agency model. It was a learning journey with stops, starts and recalibrations, as much of this was new to the primarily young team.

As the bench strength of the philanthropy and marketing teams grew, we became more successful at living our operating principles, which were built on our core values of respect, excellence, transparency and fun.

Our Philanthropy and Marketing Teams' Operating Principles:

1) Provide exemplary customer service.
2) Think strategically before executing.
3) Say yes to everyone, especially when brand awareness is low.
4) Provide 360-degree partnership opportunities that transcend the almighty dollar.

In 2005, NTFB embarked on its first capital campaign to fund the warehouse renovation that would enhance distribution efficiencies. Co-chairs Liz Minyard Lokey and Frank Roby completed the campaign in two years, raising $4.5 million against the goal of $4.2 million. Even more fitting, the end of the campaign coincided with the Food Bank's twenty-fifth anniversary celebration. That renovation was the spark responsible for the subsequent rapid growth of NTFB. A renovated volunteer space with high-voltage lights and meaningful murals enticed growing numbers of individuals and groups to come back again and again.

Once the campaign ended in 2007, the director of development resigned to move overseas, and Jan asked if I'd add fundraising to my plate. With this, I would now be responsible for all external-facing business. As I found myself saying over and over, I said yes. While I didn't have a clue about how to raise money, I knew I'd figure it out by lifting the hood of the car and asking questions.

I also knew that Jan had my back.

I began by asking a lot of questions in order to learn exactly how NTFB received, recorded, acknowledged and managed the funds from the public, government grants and investments. I spent time pouring over reports from accounting, the data entry clerk and my three team members. Then, I'd ask more questions, seeking to reconcile discrepancies between reports or to understand what seemed to be inefficient record-keeping systems. I actually loved the process. I had faith in myself and knew that together we could take this raw system and expand it into a sophisticated and efficient ecosphere. It took a concerted focus on my part to keep asking questions, as I really didn't know what I didn't know. And not every staff person appreciated my curiosity. Once I felt I knew all the ways dollars flowed in, I'd learn that I should also be tracking the bulk food donations, so I could thank those donors! Yikes. There were hundreds of those donors tracked in a separate software system that never interfaced with our donor database management system. Looking into the inventory system to learn who the donors were, I'd see that their names were misspelled or not complete. How could we thank them if I did not have trusted information? And was the name in the database the true influencer to whom I should write? In most cases, no. So that required additional research. Operations staff didn't understand why I was asking for content accuracy because, as they told me, "I enter in whatever is on the delivery slip." It was apparent to me that we needed to create a better customer relationship management system and protocol that worked for this first year, and to enhance it as we went along.

That mantra served as a truth for me over sixteen years: Build a Chevy first and work up to a Lexus in your third year.

In 2005, Jan wanted NTFB to have a paid media campaign during the holiday season, the peak fundraising period. She walked into my office and said, "Billboards, Colleen." (It had the same panache as the unforgettable and iconic line from *The Graduate*: "Plastics...") She had just returned from the Greater Boston Food Bank, which was wildly successful with outdoor advertising. She wanted that for NTFB. I was on it. Within weeks, four premier local agencies were identified, three interviewed, and one was selected—Moroch. They produced a thirty-second television spot called "Hungertown," which ran on the local ABC affiliate in November and December. While several board members were nervous about its edgy "not-a-Chamber-of-Commerce feel," it generated a 42 percent year-over-year increase in volunteer hours. The next year, RSW Creative was hired to create the 2006 holiday campaign, which expanded to include billboards, radio, online, transit, in-store and television, and a pop-up experience at NorthPark Center, a favorite upscale shopping experience based in Dallas.

Soon the agency would take on more key projects, such as redesigning our website, creating graphic brands for strategic campaigns, truck wraps and a new NTFB logo. While many nonprofits at that time were not investing in paid media and creative, we knew this level of firepower was needed if we were going to transform how hunger is tackled.

Finding the best vendor partnerships is not easy. Look for the best, those who place ego aside to learn, and bring integrity and passion to the table. RSW Creative and Moroch did just that. Time and again.

Jumping into the paid media campaign was another calculated risk Jan took that continues to pay off. Each year, the campaign has increased awareness, volunteerism and food and financial donations, all of which supports the distribution of

Holiday campaign billboards worked!

Holiday campaign by RSW Creative, NTFB's stellar marketing firm

greater amounts of nutritious foods. In 2010, the holiday campaign snowballed year-over-year public support by 22 percent, and in 2011 by 36 percent. It was not uncommon for sister food banks to call me to learn how it was done, and for Feeding America to ask me to present workshops. As part of the food bank culture across the nation, we all shared our methods with each other, knowing it would lower the tide of hunger

Soon, I noticed more outdoor advertising in the Dallas and Fort Worth areas promoting various causes. Our investment in paid media had

a multiplying effect that ultimately benefited the greater good in new and unexpected places.

With the momentum of the 2005–2007 capital campaign and our two three-year strategic plans, public support, new donors and volunteers grew exponentially between 2008 and 2014. Key vendor partnerships also contributed to the impressive fundraising results, with contracts with The Lovell Group for public relations, Brad Cecil & Associates for direct response, and RSW Creative for holiday media campaigns. Their integrated, multichannel strategies played a vital role in the effectiveness of our external-facing megaphone. All three agencies collaborated well, which helped ensure a cohesive public strategy and message.

Fresh cause marketing partnerships led to point-of-sale campaigns with Schepp's Dairy, 7-Eleven, major department and grocery retailers, pro sports teams, the Dallas International Film Festival, celebrities, hotels, car dealership associations, small startups and mom and pop shops, chambers of commerce, school alumni chapters, and elegant chef-driven events hosted by icons Stephan Pyles and Kent Rathbun, among others. Stephan played a pivotal role in launching Restaurant Week, now NTFB's top fundraiser, and served on the Food Bank's capital campaign committee. Kent created the Food Bank's Taste of the Cowboys, a signature event in partnership with the Dallas Cowboys that he grew into an annual powerhouse.

People would tell us they saw the Food Bank everywhere. When the remake of the iconic TV show *Dallas* had production breaks, stars Jesse Metcalfe and his fiancée Cara Santana would volunteer sorting food and recruiting their co-stars to raise funds. Noticing other community landmarks were weather trackers for WFAA Channel 8, I called them up and they agreed to add NTFB to those ranks. My team and I were driven to pursue all opportunities, big or small.

Feeding America expanded Hunger Action Day to a monthlong focus, activating national and local messaging into one big orange-colored call to action. We aimed to turn Dallas orange. The Omni Dallas Hotel glowed orange and gave NTFB messaging to their guests; Dallas City Hall's reflecting pool was filled with AT&T branded orange beach balls. A massive orange bow was tied around the neck of the Dallas Zoo's sixty-seven-foot-tall statue of a giraffe, and NTFB sold orange pet bandanas. Volunteers would come to sort food wearing orange wigs and would leave with a fresh mandarin orange as a snack.

Top left: Authentic leaders on and off the field (L–R): Preston Pearson, Charles Haley and Chad Hennings, Taste of the Cowboys

Top right: Actor Jesse Metcalfe builds weekend food bags for kids

Bottom left: Pet lovers support NTFB (Zeke, model)

Moonshot Partnerships: Transforming Storytelling into the Fuel That Mobilized Millions

Brad Cecil, President, Brad Cecil & Associates

I first met Colleen in the mid-'90s when she worked at Leadership Network. In addition to running a startup agency helping organizations with fundraising communication, I was a volunteer pastor at a church in the Dallas-Fort Worth area. In that role, Leadership Network invited me to join some conversations on the future of the Church and I was asked to write an article for their publication. Through that process I met Colleen. I was a fan from the beginning.

In 2003, I received a call from Colleen as she had just joined the team at the North Texas Food Bank. She asked me, "Does your firm help nonprofit organizations with direct response fundraising communication?" I informed her, "Yes, it is one of our specialties," but I also shared that "I believe in a narrative approach, not merely numbers, so I'm not sure if we're a good fit." Later I met with Colleen and Jan Pruitt to explain that if we really want the Food Bank communication to inspire people, we have to extract the stories of the people who are transformed by this work. Colleen and Jan listened to my philosophy and Jan stated simply, "If it raises money, we agree. Just show me the money."

This new approach in fundraising communication for the Food Bank in direct mail, newsletters and online did inspire people and the base of support grew. As Colleen states in this book, annual public support grew from $2.6 million per year in 2004 to $17.9 million per year in 2018, the database grew from seven thousand records to almost half a million records in that time.

This remarkable growth was due in large part to the insightful leadership of Colleen and her team at the Food Bank and the dedicated staff at Brad Cecil & Associates, Inc., working in partnership to take full advantage of the opportunity before us and paying close attention to the details of excellent database marketing.

Moonshot Partnerships: Transforming Storytelling into the Fuel That Mobilized Millions (Cont.)

In 2015, BCA was honored to be selected by the Food Bank as counsel for their capital campaign to raise $55 million to implement a new strategic vision. Having worked alongside Colleen and Jan for over ten years I looked forward to working together on this historic venture. The campaign plan was to raise $55 million—$25 million for a new distribution center, $5 million to renovate the administration building in Farmers Market, $1 million for technology to better understand the needs of the people served and $24 million to invest in partner agencies to increase their capacity.

I have been involved in elaborate campaigns but not one in which money is raised to give away. We knew that strategic plans only work if partner agencies increase capacity, and I thought this would be our biggest challenge in the campaign. Little did I know what was ahead. The campaign was off to a great start but soon Jan Pruitt started feeling ill. We hoped it was temporary but when the diagnosis of cancer came, everyone was devastated. This is the point where Colleen stepped up to a new leadership role. She was determined to see this campaign completed. Colleen made a promise to Jan that her vision would become reality.

On January 3, 2017, Jan passed away. A year later in January 2018 we received word that we had in fact secured our final gift for the campaign and exceeded our $55 million goal! Many, many great leaders contributed to this success of the campaign—Pam and John Beckert, the Perot family, the Moody and Mabee Foundations, Alliance Data, Toyota North America and many more, but I will never forget the leadership Colleen displayed when the going got tough and we had every excuse to quit.

Moonshot Partnerships: Transforming Storytelling into the Fuel that Mobilized Millions
(Cont.)

The great Indian leader, Mahatma Gandhi, said, "There are people in the world so hungry, that God cannot appear to them except in the form of bread."

Over the past 15 years BCA has partnered with the Food Bank to raise a combined $93 million, over $37 million in annual fund support and over $55 million in capital. What a joy to partner with Colleen in this remarkable work and all to transform the lives of hungry people, people in need, often without hope.

www.CecilCommunication.com

Moonshot Partnerships: Choosing a PR Partner that Embraces Brand Strategy
Betty Lovell, APR, President, The Lovell Group

The year was 2003, and the North Texas Food Bank (NTFB) was seeking a PR partner to play a pivotal role during its most critical time of year—holiday fundraising. There was a catch: NTFB had no budget. As a boutique PR firm, we historically did not take on pro bono clients. However, this was different. First, I had personally supported NTFB for years and believed in its mission. I'd even recommended that certain clients select NTFB as a charity beneficiary. Secondly, when I realized that NTFB was looking to build and grow a strong brand, I saw a far greater purpose. Besides, it's difficult to say no to the very dedicated Jan Pruitt and Colleen Brinkmann! The Lovell Group (formerly Lovell PR) was fully on board! Lovell proved its bottom-line value to NTFB during that first campaign. The relationship quickly grew beyond a pro bono project to a strategic partnership where the Lovell team had an important seat at the table in raising awareness and much-needed funds for NTFB's mission.

The success of Lovell's partnership with North Texas Food Bank has been a shared commitment to growing a brand that raises significant funds to feed hungry North Texans through a distribution network of two hundred regional charities. NTFB did a masterful job bringing on the right partners, those who saw the vision and could do the work needed. For many years, The Lovell Group worked closely with RSW Creative, NTFB's creative partner, on messaging and positioning of ad campaigns, etc., that dovetail with overarching brand initiatives.

There are countless examples of our team's collective efforts, but I'd like to highlight two of the key campaigns we have been pivotal in growing for NTFB for well over a decade.

Moonshot Partnerships: Choosing a PR Partner that Embraces Brand Strategy (Cont.)

Holiday Campaigns/Capital Campaigns

For many nonprofit organizations, the holidays are a traditionally busy time. In fact, the North Texas Food Bank often aims to raise 50 percent of its annual donations from Thanksgiving to New Year's Day. My firm engaged local media and potential donors using an integrated, multitiered communications strategy that leveraged NTFB ads and promotions. Lovell's team also creatively positioned fundraising needs with personal stories—the real and moving stories of hunger among our neighbors—and continually refreshed this over the years. The annual effort included a campaign launch event and multiple media and community events to showcase the Food Bank's hands-on work in the North Texas community.

The Lovell Group crafted unique campaign elements and messaging that kept the efforts fresh and relevant each year—from a Holiday Giving Guide showcasing how contributions met tangible needs for NTFB to highlighting the potential impacts of timely legislation. Lovell remained focused on keeping NTFB top of mind in news stories, social media channels and targeted community outreach to prevent thousands of North Texans from going without food at a time of year often characterized by family feasts.

In a single year, campaign efforts helped NTFB raise more than $7.5 million in holiday gifts—representing continued annual increases. The holiday campaign has been recognized with MarCom Gold and MarCom Platinum Awards for nonprofit communications, along with the Good to Great Marketing Campaign of the Year from Feeding America, and many others.

Moonshot Partnerships: Choosing a PR Partner that Embraces Brand Strategy (Cont.)

DFW Restaurant Week

The single largest annual fundraiser for the North Texas Food Bank is DFW Restaurant Week. With the help of The Lovell Group, DFW Restaurant Week has become North Texas' largest culinary event. The beloved foodie campaign, spearheaded by Entercom, features delicious prix fixe menus at more than 150 of the area's hottest restaurants. The event not only fills seats during the historically slow summer dining season, it also channels 20 percent of the proceeds from each meal to two local nonprofits, North Texas Food Bank in the Dallas area and Lena Pope in Tarrant County.

The Lovell Group has had a seat at the table for fifteen years and counting. My firm's involvement has included brand building, campaign management, media relations and social media initiatives. Lovell ensures that it is widely covered in local and regional media. Through strategic partnerships and marketing promotions with high-profile national brands as sponsors, Lovell has continued to help build credibility and notoriety for this popular event. Recent focus has included strengthening the brand across traditional and social media platforms, as well as evolving the program to appeal to a broader demographic. Last year alone, the campaign raised nearly $800,000 for these two nonprofits.

www.thelovellgroupinc.com

Branding Your Strategic Plan Pays Off

Two three-year, back-to-back strategic plans propelled NTFB forward into a new stratosphere of public engagement and impact. *Close the Gap* (2009–2011) would accelerate annual distribution from 26 million meals to the then-current need of 50 million. *Rethink Hunger* focused on healthier, smarter and stronger solutions to hunger, not quantity. It was vital to reinvent the organization in order to provide healthier food to those in need

Most organizations consider strategic plans operational blueprints, and that's undoubtedly true. However, with just that mind-set, you're leaving a lot of high-octane fuel in the tank. By creating a sub-brand for the strategic plan, you are leveraging it as a marketing and fundraising asset. When positioned correctly with your organization's core brand and message, there is an alignment and a compelling call to action, and it further serves as a way to energize your whole team, paid and unpaid, to achieve the plan.

Adding a cohesive graphic icon (that syncs with your organization's logo and brand) is just the start. Develop key messages, talking points for media/public speaking, brand personality factors and a style guide. Train the organization's leadership team and staff, the board, other essential volunteers and your team to speak to this plan. Infuse the messaging points of the strategic plan into digital and printed collateral. Create a microsite with a toolbox of materials volunteers can easily download, share and use.

Without branding *Close the Gap*, we could not have doubled public support from **$6 million to $12 million in three years**. The same principle applies to *Rethink Hunger*.

Rethink Hunger.
Bringing Better Solutions to the Table

My goal for both strategic plans was for the public and NTFB supporters to feel a different sort of energy when they walked through the door, so they would know that we were *Closing the Gap* or *Rethinking Hunger*. At the very least, they would exit back into their world knowing that (a) the Food Bank was doing something different, and (b) it was smart and would help those at the front lines of need.

Because this was a new approach for Food Bank managers, I went department by department, asking to speak briefly at their internal staff meetings where I could provide the FAQ and request they brand their external documents for the timespan of the plan. Plastic boxes were placed in each truck cab with easy-to-use collateral and inexpensive giveaways that drivers could gift to their contacts when picking up bulk food donations. Talking points were given to the agency relations team so they could educate the two hundred partner agencies on the plan, further ensuring that our message would fan out to the grass tops and grassroots. For the first time, selected key vendors were approached to support NTFB through volunteerism, in kind and financially. Four- and five-figure gifts began to arrive, and over the years vendor support has been steady, even when NTFB is not a customer, all because of our focus. Volunteers would leave with a colorful round branded sticker on their shirt that read, "I helped feed thousands today by Rethinking Hunger."

In sum, we wanted everyone who entered the NTFB airspace to tattoo into their consciousness our strategic plan mission, be it *Close the Gap* or *Rethink Hunger*. Everything seemed to flow from these branding initiatives, which played a pivotal role in expanding the Food Bank's brand.

"I don't know of anyone who brands strategic plans, but we do," exclaimed Jan proudly.

*A check presentation with NTFB Marketing Director
Sayeda Mahler with donors*

This focused effort on branding, cause marketing and paid media paid off as revenue increased year after year. Additionally, fundraising, marketing and communication efforts were recognized regionally and nationally with awards from Feeding America and PR associations.

Growth in Public Support (During Strategic Plan Years)

Strategic Plan	Fiscal Year	Total Public Support
	2008	$6,275,000
Close the Gap, Year 1	2009	$9,915,000
Close the Gap, Year 2	2010	$11,619,000
Close the Gap, Year 3	2011	$12,875,000
Rethink Hunger, Year 1	2012	$16,884,000
Rethink Hunger, Year 2	2013	$16,279,000
Rethink Hunger, Year 3	2014	$17,626,000

Personal Application #3

Keep in my mind my mantra--start small and scale up. Even if your organization is a year away from launching a strategic plan, or you've already started it, dive in by thinking through and implementing some of these deliverables. It will make a difference in the net outcome of your public support efforts. Having a secondary message tucked underneath the umbrella of your organization's core message does not confuse people. Keep your messaging simple, tight and consistent. Remind your team that this new message will garner greater response from prospects, donors, the media and community leaders. People love to be part of something new and special.

Checklist for a Branded Strategic Plan

- ❏ Host idea session to determine the "personality, look and feel" of the plan, core message points, target audiences, fundraising and marketing objectives, and timeline.
- ❏ With your team, create an integrated marketing and fundraising plan, with a timeline, that informs, educates and offers a call to action, with measurable goals for success.
- ❏ Create a case for support (long and short versions).
- ❏ Obtain a logo that aligns itself with your organization's primary logo and brand.
- ❏ Add to your organization's style guide a section that features your strategic plan's logo, brand personality and placement guidelines.
- ❏ Create branded communications materials (print, digital) for external and internal use:
  - ❏ Fact sheet
  - ❏ Public speaking template speech

❑ FAQ
❑ Other
❑ Create a branded microsite; include relevant materials that inform, educate and elicit a call to action.
  ❑ Include a toolbox of user-friendly materials for public use.
❑ Equip staff, board, core volunteers, partners and key vendors to be effective champions of the plan outcomes.
❑ As needed, create target-specific communications tools for children's, youth, faith, civic and academic groups.

Each year we'd analyze the required staff skills and either add positions, promote or redesign the organizational chart. While results were impressive, we were growing so fast that the size and bench strength of the team could not keep pace with the ambitious annual goals and the incoming levels of public interest. Marketing, development managers and I were stretched thin, covering too many desks. Support roles were few. Turnover was high, and NTFB did not yet have HR programs for professional development, management 101, retention and recognition. And a recent market study on compensation made it painfully clear: we could not compete with the salaries offered by larger organizations in town. The day we lost a valuable gift officer to a prestigious healthcare institution informed me of two things—one positive (our brand was strong) and one negative (our compensation packages needed review, or else we'd continue to bleed talent).

Jan's reputation as a highly active change agent was growing. She was now being tapped across Texas and beyond. At the national level, Jan served on the board of Feeding America, and later as board chair. She also led the search for a new CEO of Feeding America in 2005 and was their interim COO for a year. While serving as their interim COO, Jan asked Paul Wunderlich, NTFB's COO by this time, and myself to step in and handle the day-to-day decision-making while she commuted weekly between Chicago and Dallas. More and more struggling food banks would turn to Jan for guidance. And she would help.

The pace continued to pick up at the Food Bank. I had remarried and my husband Barney was an endless source of strength and encouragement.

Freedom is not worth having if it does not include the freedom to make mistakes.

– Mahatma Gandhi

Some of Our Best Achievements Emerged from Mistakes

Seriously true.

We had more than one hundred community-led third-party events that raised food, funds and awareness, many growing in impact. An additional twenty were "our events," which were complex and logistically heavy, but well attended. While at a national meeting with food bank peers, I learned that most of my colleagues only planned for two to three events in their budget, allowing the community to run with the rest. I called back to the office and asked Marketing Manager Sayeda Mahler for the average gross revenue from the twenty events we produced. She said she'd check and call me right back.

"Around $2,000," she responded. Yikes.

Within a month, Sayeda, a young professional advancing on a meteoric trajectory at the Food Bank, had developed an action plan that reallocated resources, so staff only produced three key events a year, and the others were either mothballed or given to an external community group to manage.

Events, a costly way to fundraise, are successful when viewed as a marketing strategy:

1) Strategically designed for a target audience;
2) Focused on providing a customized memorable experience; and
3) Built on measurable outcomes with annual growth projections.

Determine your target audience and their preferences, core values, what incentivizes them, what you're seeking from their participation, and the outcomes. State the objectives and measurable goals clearly so the team is in sync. Then build it according to that strategic plan. An event that is beautifully planned and executed but has no underpinning strategy is a costly misstep. Successful events advance the mission when they provide the target audience with a uniquely meaningful experience that then leads to trackable action. Strive for that one-of-a-kind experience.

On another occasion, one of our top corporate billion-dollar brand partners stopped me in the parking lot after an event planning meeting to gently but firmly inform me that my team needed to perform at a higher level. She added that they only partner with two charities, NTFB being one, and they regularly receive inquiries from at least twenty charities a month seeking their help. She didn't want to lose NTFB but needed a higher level of performance by my team—now. I got it. Within hours I shared this message with Sayeda, who listened intently, was never defensive, and immediately assured me she would take care of it.

"I'm on it," she said. "Consider it done."

The next day she met with her team, conveyed the donor's concerns and her faith that together they could meet expectations. She gave specific examples of what needed to be improved immediately and within thirty days. Because of her management style and the mutual respect among the team, they were able to quickly recalibrate. It was a good reminder not to take external relationships for granted, and to always strive for excellence in customer service.

Over the years, this corporate donor and I have reflected on what we call our "parking lot conversation," glad that there was a good outcome for all parties. I was fortunate to have a strong leader-manager in Sayeda, a marketing team that was adaptable and a donor who cared enough to be direct. Within weeks I was able to convey back to Sayeda that the donor was pleased with the progress.

Both experiences exemplify the importance of developing (and nourishing) strong leader-managers and building trusted donor relationships that can survive a "parking lot conversation."

Personal Application #4

Take a few minutes to reflect on mistakes you've made (of any size), both in the workplace and in life. Without a doubt, my best learnings have emerged from missteps, massive challenges and moving too quickly without giving time for "the tea leaves to soak." What would you do if presented with the opportunity for a do-over? What resources would you need to equip yourself for success?

After the *Rethink Hunger* strategic plan ended in 2014, fundraising leveled off, primarily due to the competing $55 million capital campaign that was coming up around the curve. Public support stood at **$18.1 million in 2015** and, as we'd see over the next three years, **the capital campaign caused an ebb and flow that impacted our ability to achieve our annual fund goals**. The way we raised funds had understandably become more strategic and complex, requiring sophisticated leadership, talent and experience at all levels. We added greater capacity in research, data management and support services. New initiatives filled our days: our Major Gift Program and Pam Beckert's Letter Writing Campaign were generating new donors and greater revenue year after year; preparation for our massive capital campaign was in full swing.

Board strength was exceptional. And NTFB was now attracting support from philanthropists previously involved in the arts, academia and healthcare. We had moved our external-facing offices to the Dallas Farmers Market, which made it easier to meet with donors and gain visibility. The donor database had grown from seven thousand records in 2003 to nearly five hundred thousand by 2017. Our Major Gift Program was growing, so we raised the bar for how we defined a major gift from $2,500 to $10,000, and NTFB received two unsolicited seven-figure gifts for annual operations. Soon, an $800,000 bequest followed from a donor who had donated $100 each month the previous couple of years. In order for me to focus primarily on fundraising, Brett Gray was hired as chief marketing officer to oversee marketing, communications, public policy and the volunteer experience. His PR agency expertise was invaluable as we focused on crisis management, reshaping our brand and raising greater amounts of support.

The high growth period of the past decade required everyone to be adaptable and open to change. Those who weren't wired that way or found it uncomfortable left. The organizational pressure impacted retention across all departments. This is why, over and over, I emphasize the vital importance of an organization investing in professional HR expertise—be it internal, consulting or strategic support among the board of directors.

As leaders who are focused on brand and relationship building, we are "selling" something intangible. What we are offering someone is the opportunity to invest in our mission, which will, in turn, provide a greater sense of wellbeing to them, their family, their community and their workplace. That's not an easy sell, as competition, preferences and free will can get in the way. When placed in the right space, with the right leadership and team, people and communities step up. I've seen it time and again. I'm sure you have as well. When focused on creating the correct value proposition, good happens. The courtship of relationship building requires artful patience, active listening and pure authenticity. It must flow from your deepest reservoir of passion for the mission.

Personal Application #5

List the top one or two reasons why each of the target markets below would desire to invest voice, time, in kind and financially to further your organization's mission.

#1 – Target Market: Individuals, Families

Voice	
Time	
In Kind	
Finances	

#2 – Target Market: Children, Youth, Students, Alumni Groups

Voice	
Time	
In Kind	
Finances	

#3 – Target Market: Seniors

Voice	
Time	
In Kind	
Finances	

#4 – Target Market: Businesses, Corporations, Startups, Newly Relocated (Leadership, Board, Employees and Their Clients)

Voice	
Time	
In Kind	
Finances	

#5 – Target Market: Young Professionals

Voice	
Time	
In Kind	
Finances	

#6 – Target Market: Foundations, Staff, Trustees and Other Stakeholders

Voice	
Time	
In Kind	
Finances	

#7 – Target Market: Faith Communities; Civic and Grassroots Groups

Voice	
Time	
In Kind	
Finances	

Once you've completed that, how does your organization measure up against these aspirations you've jotted down? Are there strategies and tactics in place to operationalize all these ideas? Perhaps some, but not all? Conduct an audit. Hold an internal focus group of staff and get their input on what endeavors need to be retired, restarted, reframed or created from the ground up. Piloting a new strategy is a smart way to launch a program. Test it out. Tweak and launch. While we were proud to be known as a large, fearless organization, the higher the goals, the higher the risk. The pedestal upon which we had initially stepped on was now a lot taller. Falling off could now hurt. As NTFB grew, we also relished opportunities to pilot ideas and programs before rolling them out. Make sure your outreach is designed to appeal to your various audiences in an authentic, low-cost manner.

It's a Volunteer Experience, Not a Program

In today's world, our most valued commodity is time. With a focus on building and operating a vibrant volunteer experience, an organization can leverage it as a dynamic megaphone that grows the support base and annual revenue.

Best volunteer experience in town!

Now let me clarify, because you may assume that just because someone gives a gift of their time they should be ready to contribute financially. Studies have shown that this assumption is false. Certainly, a well-managed volunteer experience with skillful cultivation and stewardship leads to deeper relationships. Volunteering alone does not serve as qualification for a financial gift. More work must be done by gift officers and other key relationship builders to make that happen.

Today, the Food Bank's volunteer experience is one of North Texas' most popular opportunities for service. Over forty-six thousand experiences have been contributed. One experience equates to a two-and-a-half-hour shift.

When I arrived at NTFB in 2002, I found a volunteer program that was well intentioned, but on autopilot. Each week, one to two hundred volunteers would box and sort with minimal orientation or follow-up. A year later, Jan asked me to oversee the program. I could see all possibilities, and it energized me. We had this great opportunity to create a premier hub of community and service that would attract people of all ages, faiths, ZIP codes, occupations, genders, races and political persuasions. We could design it to be efficient, motivational and impactful, and give the volunteer a sense of fulfillment as they departed. If we did that well and consistently, we could play a role in building a strong North Texas. We had a massive open warehouse. We had racks and pallets of food that needed to be broken down into smaller bundles for agency pickup. Hunger was a core human need, something we all understood. And no matter how one votes or worships, everyone agrees that hunger is unacceptable. We could create unique volunteer experiences throughout the year tied to holidays, themes, faith and cultural celebrations, and host birthdays for kids, bar and bat mitzvahs, and Eid celebrations.

We worked through some thorny issues with operations, since we needed their staff to manage the quality control of the volunteer lines and collaborate with our volunteer coordinator. In due course they understood the value volunteers brought beyond the free labor force and we were off and running. Because my four- to five-person team was stretched covering marketing, events, communications, direct mail and now the volunteer program, the full transformation of the volunteer experience took five years.

The "starter fuel" that propelled NTFB's volunteer experience into today's greatness was the arrival of Lydia Rudy, a smart and passionate recent college graduate, in 2008. No matter how difficult the hurdles, she had a can-do spirit. Lydia reinvented the 360-degree process used for signing up, orientation, volunteering and acknowledging that had served NTFB for years.

It's valuable to schedule an annual audit of your volunteer experience, step by step. Make sure processes and roles are aligned and operating clearly. Ultimately, you want each volunteer to leave feeling grateful for the opportunity you've given them: to use their hands to better the world. Exemplary customer service should drive your strategies and brand. Strive to exceed expectations by sending a personal note or email to a volunteer group leader to share with their team. Send a thank you via one of your social media channels.

One of the most exciting innovations witnessed in recent years was when Jennifer Green was hired to run the NTFB volunteer experience. Gifted with project management, strategy and theatrical abilities, Jennifer transformed the informational orientation into a cheer-driven, high-energy experience for the tens of thousands who volunteered annually. She took ownership of the whole program, building strong cross-departmental relationships and making smart hires for her team. Every volunteer experience needs a leader like that.

Continually analyze for ways to use volunteer labor as your organization morphs and grows. I don't know of any nonprofit that has an endless budget; we're always tasked with doing more with less. So, leverage that wisely. Create a cadre of dedicated, well-trained volunteers who can be your extended team. Send them out for check presentations, speaking engagements and informational fairs.

In 2004, I launched our first volunteer leadership program––Hunger Ambassadors. We were saying yes to every opportunity and needed extra staff. Since our budget didn't support that additional expense, this cadre of polished volunteers served as unpaid staff. Trained and equipped with updated materials and knowledge, we'd dispatch them to check presentations and staff informational tables at corporate fairs, and had them participate in our Speakers Bureau. Twice a year we'd host a breakfast or lunch during which they'd get updated information and training, and once a year we'd host an appreciation happy hour and gift them complimentary event tickets. The group grew from twelve to twenty-five in a year, most of them retirees and working professionals seeking opportunities where they could "dig deeper" in terms of contributing. Each was given a name badge and logo wear and listed on the website. When well organized and managed, this model does not require much staff support. In fact, consider selecting a volunteer to lead the group and train their successor after they complete a two-year term.

Unfortunately, the Hunger Ambassador program was not sustainable after five years. Demands to fulfill our core fundraising goals were intense, and staffing within this area was fractured. The team only had so much firepower; there wasn't the capacity to shoulder the program effectively. It was disappointing because it did bring measurable value. However, in ambitious, high-growth organizations priorities shift. One must be adaptable and look out for the well-being of the team. Though our program didn't last, Houston Food Bank's did. They have an outstanding volunteer leadership program called Apple Corps, which I highly recommend looking into.

Once your primary volunteer program is developed and running smoothly, consider creating affinity groups consisting of like-minded communities. Strategically decide which ones you want to create based on target markets that can benefit your organization. These new voices and hands can become powerful advocates, fundraisers and volunteer leaders.

In 2013 we identified five target markets that possessed values associated with volunteerism, family, basic human needs and faith: LGBTQA+, Jewish, Indian American and two high-wealth neighborhoods in Dallas. We believed that by targeting some of our communications, marketing, donor outreach and stewardship, we could measurably increase support (of all kinds) from each of these groups. To do this right, we needed to learn more about where they lived, worshipped, what media they read and the donor profile (household income, marital status, ZIP codes, etc.) This is a fairly low-cost and easy way to grow your support base.

Soon, we were hosting bar and bat mitzvahs, and youth were donating their gift money to the Food Bank. A leading synagogue dedicated their annual festival to NTFB and invited us to speak during their services. Resounding Harmony, a one-hundred-voice chorus, supported NTFB for three years and performed before volunteers in our warehouse; and by 2017, the Food Bank sponsored a float in the Dallas Pride Parade. An Indian-American Council gained momentum when the right co-chairs were found—Anna and Raj Asava, a Plano-based couple with remarkable energy and leadership. Young Professionals was also launched, but after two years of lagging results it did not take off until the right leader stepped in—Brent Beckert, a young attorney who has built a model program that brings new energy, awareness and financial support through monthly activities. A board alumni group was formed five years ago as a way to keep interested board members engaged. New co-chairs are selected by outgoing co-chairs to serve a two-year term, and annual goals for event attendance, introductions and fundraising are set by the group, which meets three times a year. It's a vibrant and engaged group with deep roots in the Food Bank.

Do not be discouraged if your new affinity group program does not take off right away. It requires the right volunteer leadership, coupled with streamlined staff support. Find your "Asavas" or "Brent Beckert."

Personal Application #6

Host a small focus group or conduct an informal survey with diverse volunteers (age, the frequency of volunteering, longevity with the organization, gender, background, intent behind volunteering). Learn what works, what doesn't and what are the unmet needs.

Increasingly, people are seeking more meaning in their lives, ways to unplug from technology and use their hands to see and feel the impact of their gift of time. You hold the power to open that door for your community. What are some ways your volunteer experience can be enhanced and serve more needs of the organization without increased costs? With the influx of Baby Boomers retiring, what needs does your organization have that can align with this valuable demographic who come with wisdom and life skills?

Moonshot Leadership: Jan

I had reached out to Charles Pruitt so this book could also include insights into Jan's impact on making good happen. He and daughter Natalie invited Barney and me over for burgers, wine and conversation to discuss just that.

Charles and Jan met in high school in Ennis, Texas, and raised four remarkable children. They were a close-knit family. As a stay-at-home mom, she volunteered at St. Vincent de Paul and then stepped into her first nonprofit job as director of the newly formed Lancaster Outreach, which provided an array of human services, including food and counseling. While there, she earned her bachelor's degree in social work from Dallas Baptist University. After eleven years, she became director of the Texas Food Bank Association, and two years later was hired to lead the North Texas Food Bank.

Jan had applied twice to be director of NTFB but was turned down the first time. "She didn't have the corporate look they were seeking," explained Natalie. It was providential that Jan was not hired at that time, as soon after a massive tornado hit Lancaster and her organization was called upon to provide relief for the tens of thousands impacted. The skills she learned during that season of disaster relief would serve her well in the coming years.

During her twenty years at the North Texas Food Bank, her leadership style expanded in response to the hunger crisis in North Texas and America. Often described as "fearless," "authentic" and "visionary," Jan inspired nonprofit leaders locally and within the national food bank network.

Moonshot Leadership: Jan (Cont.)

Jan's Eleven Abiding Principles

By Charles, Eryk, Natalie, Chris and Jonathan Pruitt

1. Be authentic and continually inspire your team.
2. Treat everyone with equal respect, regardless of their station in life.
3. Express thanks in a timely and genuine way, because nothing happens in a silo.
4. Get control of the organization. Get the right people in the right roles so you can then do your job as the leader. Recognize potential and invest in helping them reach the next level. For others, help them move on.
5. Build a loyal and trusted executive team that has your back.
6. Be accessible. Give out your mobile number. It will directly impact the organization's brand. *(Jan was known to say yes to 4 a.m. media interviews or key opportunities that fell on a holiday.)*
7. Do it right.
8. "No" was not the right answer. Bring a solution.
9. Don't be afraid to ask questions and try new things.
10. Have strong family support.
11. Most importantly, believe in yourself.

Moonshot Leadership: Jan (Cont.)

Growing up, I found no more valuable advice than what I received from my mother, Jan Pruitt, as she led us both by example and wisdom after pursuing her own ambitious dreams. This book preserves her advice in amber for future leaders, visionaries and dreamers of this generation and those to come. It's the perfect reflection of the legacy of a woman who built teams from individuals, brought solutions to problems and elevated everyone around her to get the job done. Reading it is like hearing my mother's voice again, over my shoulder.

Eryk Pruitt, Award-winning Author, Filmmaker,
and Producer (of The Long Dance*)*

If you're offered a seat on a rocket ship, don't ask what seat! Just get on.

– Sheryl Sandberg

A Case Study: Achieving *Stop Hunger Build Hope*, a Three-Year, $55 Million Capital Campaign (Against All Odds)

Stop Hunger Build Hope was the largest capital campaign by a social service organization in North Texas. That alone makes it historic. What elevates it to a case study is its complexity, its goal and the way it was achieved against insurmountable odds. A remarkable team of paid and unpaid leaders and heroes powered ahead with moral courage, servant leadership, dedication and care.

Here is the story.

On Thursday, January 18, 2018, the North Texas Food Bank made history. That afternoon, final commitments flowed in, taking us over the $55 million finish line. Our new CEO, Trisha Cunningham, played a pivotal role in securing the last $4+ million. A total of $55,685,380 (101 percent) was confirmed with five hundred thirty-six gifts from individuals, foundations, corporations and organizations.

Staff throughout the building gathered in the conference room, and we dialed in Co-chairs Pam and John Beckert, Board Chair Anurag Jain and the board of directors. It was a surreal moment for everyone. While the journey had been brutal at times, we experienced our share of high moments, and this one was the sweetest! We had just planted the flag on *our* Everest.

Four months into the campaign in 2015, Jan Pruitt was diagnosed with cancer. This was an earth-shattering blow to the organization, close-knit staff and community. Eighteen months later she would pass away, leaving a lasting legacy of service. Jan and the board's vision was to close the gap by increasing annual output from 62 million nutritious meals to the current need of 92 million by 2025, a ten-year runway. With the capital campaign over, NTFB would now tackle its next significant milestone— implementing the three-pillar strategic plan: Community Engagement, Network Expansion and Client Visibility.

Katherine and Eric Reeves, along with Katherine's four siblings, contributed the $10 million lead campaign gift. This tribute gift honoring their grandmother, Lula Mae Perot, and their aunt, Bette Perot, exemplified the family's multigenerational focus on feeding the hungry, which started with Lula Mae feeding the homeless from her kitchen door in Texarkana, Texas. Bette and the Perot Family Foundation had provided the Food Bank's only distribution center, and the new distribution facility in Plano would be named the Perot Family Campus.

Katherine's passion expanded well beyond her role as a board leader when she mobilized significant support from her family and friends. In 2013, Eric and Katherine's niece, Stella, and her best friend, Quinn, created a successful and scalable annual holiday fundraiser called Jingle Bell Mistletoe (with the social media hashtag #KissAndTella), selling mistletoe to raise funds for NTFB. Over the five years of the campaign it generated $131,081, which provided over three hundred thousand nutritious meals. What incredible vision and impact these elementary school-age leaders had!

In preparation for the campaign in early 2015, Jan asked me to focus primarily on the capital campaign, but only if I felt my team could continue raising the annual fund, budgeted between **$17 and $18.5 million for each of the three years**. I knew my team could handle it because of their tenure, commitment and talent, and each assured me they were "in" for the journey. What we were facing would require shoulder-to-shoulder strength from the CEO, board, executive team, fundraising and the other external-facing teams. This nationally recognized, award-winning team was committing to a three-year trek to the summit of *our* Mt. Everest––a height we had yet to conquer. My goals were to achieve the capital campaign on schedule, ensure the team remained energized and valued, and simultaneously raise the annual fund goals. If done right, North Texans would step up and donate more **$110 million in the next three years**.

By the spring of 2015, the capital campaign consultant had been selected and feasibility meetings were complete. Results indicated that our community and relationships would support a $55 million capital campaign. We were ready.

Stella and Quinn, inspiring leaders

(L–R) NTFB leader Jeffrey King and me with Katherine Perot Reeves.

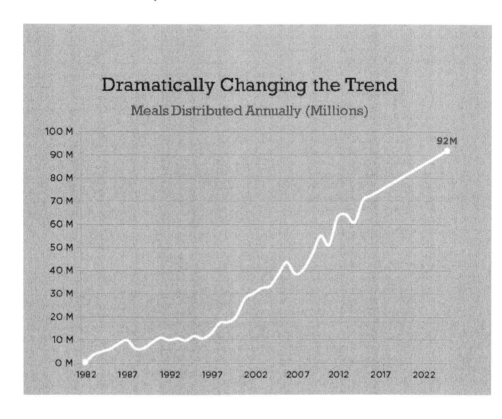

Seven Key Factors That Achieve a Historic Capital Campaign:

1. **A smart, defensible strategic plan will garner support.**

   Time and again when meeting with prospects and donors, they would remark that our intent to provide access to 92 million nutritious meals by 2025 was "a smart, well-thought-out and forward-thinking plan." For those who were more cautious, their trust in Jan and the board carried them forward. Others were impressed by those serving on the planning committee, a group of brilliant strategists and critical thinkers consisting of current and former board members. Our consultant created engaging communications tools that included the case for support, the summary of the plan, and easy-to-read charts and visuals.

2. **Your CEO is the No. 1 fundraiser and face of the organization.**

While we know this, it bears emphasizing. In the fast-moving, demanding pace of most nonprofits it is easy for leadership to relegate media appearances to a communications liaison. Other than a few special cases, most media interviews merit the CEO. This helps increase their name and visual recognition. With a well-known CEO, everything else flows more seamlessly—from securing meetings with major donor prospects to closing significant gifts. That, in turn, translates into greater public support of all kinds. Investing in a one-day media training is often needed and is invaluable.

3. **Engaged boards ensure campaign success.**

Before the launch of the campaign, each board member made a personal campaign pledge in place of their annual fund gift. While this created a challenge for the staff fundraising team, since they'd have to backfill this lost annual revenue with other incremental giving, it was powerful to inform campaign prospects that 100 percent of our board was investing in this campaign and plan. Board members continued to support the organization by attending events and contributing smaller annual gifts. In the final six months, several board members generously extended their campaign pledges for another year. It's important to keep the board informed of campaign progress and areas that need help, such as asking for introductions to people and organizations who are on your list of potential donors. A monthly "Who Do You Know" email is an efficient way to poll the board and campaign committee. While board members are experts in their professions, fundraising is often a mystery and can be intimidating. Assure them that their help can span from an email or phone call introduction to joining you at an appointment. Let them know that the staff and co-chairs stand ready to provide them with all the tools they need to be successful.

Needing an extra boost in the final six months of our campaign, our co-chairs issued a board challenge to raise $500,000 in ninety days to secure the naming rights of a pantry as a tribute to Jan Pruitt. More than $800,000 was contributed, with gifts ranging from $100 to $500,000. Offering the board a unique, package-ready campaign within a campaign, complete with collateral material, talking points and an emotive benefit (i.e., the naming of the pantry in memory of the former CEO) is a strong way to engage them, bring in new donors and get you closer to the goal. This is a model opportunity for any organization and board.

4. **Campaign leadership and teams require dedicated focus and adaptability.**

The appropriate staff lead for a capital campaign is the EVP of development or the chief philanthropy officer. Depending on the goal size, this leader should give serious consideration to (a) how much time they can dedicate just to the campaign and (b) if their direct reports and other staff can shoulder more responsibilities during the campaign. Identify who can serve as the campaign manager; ideally this is someone who is detail oriented, with strong leadership and project skills. If a new position is added, keep in mind that once the campaign is over, the person and duties can segue into a gift officer role to steward and cultivate new donors whose first gift was through the capital campaign. Most likely, there will be a few hundred new donors to encourage. Capital campaigns are complicated and come with high risk due to the type of donor you're approaching. Make sure everyone on your team and the organization's leadership are informed of the campaign framework, timeline and your expectations. It's essential that all employees understand the purpose of the plan and campaign and feel involved. The campaign manager must maintain the Master Gift Confirmation tracking tool, not the consultant. This list should be kept up to date on a daily basis with the donor, gift and intent (verbal, pledge or cash) information. Work closely with your finance department to design this tracking tool template so it works for both departments and includes weekly reconciliations.

5. **Selecting the right counsel is as important as the strategic plan; selecting the right campaign counsel is non-negotiable.**

Capital campaigns are daunting. They require a different rhythm, strategy and level of strength than annual fund campaigns. Thus, the need for an experienced and trustworthy consultant is imperative. I selected our campaign counsel based on the following criteria:

- Authentic respect for the organization and leadership;
- Large-market capital campaign experience raising a minimum of $10 million;
- The commitment that the senior, most experienced consultant would service our campaign; and
- Knowledge of the North Texas philanthropic landscape.

I polled fundraising peers in higher education, healthcare, social service and consulting sectors on their consulting firm recommendations. I selected four firms, issued an RFP and held interviews. Jan was clear that the decision rested with me. She would not be involved.

We chose the right counsel for our campaign: Brad Cecil & Associates. As our direct response vendor for twelve years, they had an unbeaten track record of delivering on their promises. There was so much to do on a daily and weekly basis that before long Brad, his senior consultant Vickie Mathews and coordinator Helen O'Connor were considered part of the staff team, with access to internal resources. They provided guidance as we navigated the fluidity associated with Jan's absence.

It is imperative that the consultant and nonprofit possess mutual **respect**, **passion** and **commitment**. Without these three elements, nothing can occur. A capital campaign—even with the CEO in place—is a complex, challenging endeavor that will require you to have difficult conversations with counsel along the way.

6. **Recruiting the right co-chairs is non-negotiable.**

Pam and John Beckert are, and will remain, my heroes. They put their personal lives on hold for over three years to lead this ambitious campaign amid all the twists, turns and hurdles. Look for leaders who possess longevity, loyalty and love for the organization, and who are avid champions of the strategic plan. Without question, they should be some of your community's most respected leaders. Don't twist arms, as chairing a campaign is time consuming and difficult. However, assure them of the strength of the organization's brand, CEO (whom they should already be aware of), board of directors, fundraising track record and the support they'll receive from staff and counsel. Find ways to genuinely deepen your relationship with the co-chairs and build systems that respect their communication and business preferences. Create communication protocols for staff, co-chairs and the committee. Less is always best, and accuracy and timeliness are paramount. Use these touchpoints to inform, update and salute. Generally speaking, the CEO and executive fundraiser should be the primary communicators to the co-chairs. No matter how bad the news is on any issue, convey it in a timely, honest manner. Be confident of your perspectives, even if they are divergent to the co-chairs', and share them in a respectful, self-assured way.

7. **Campaign committees add momentum and name-brand cachet.**

A campaign committee of twenty-five to thirty-five households (individual or couples) was the optimum size for a campaign of this magnitude in a large metroplex. A committee should include critical founders, former board members and key supporters that represent the early, middle and present years. Create a wish list of fifty or more people and cull it down with the right voices around the table: CEO, campaign co-chairs, board chair, founders, fundraising leadership and gift officers. Seek diversity in all its definitions: history with the organization, tenure, size of support, age, gender, geography, professional expertise, ethnicity, faith and name recognition. Keep in mind the "one-third rule"—one-third will be highly active, one-third will generate one or two gifts or connections, and one-third will be in name only. Create clear expectations for committee members, which should include a personal campaign commitment of any size, attendance at meetings, and assistance with introductions and the securing of gifts. Include the campaign timeline and schedule of meetings.

Our NTFB committee meetings consisted of a monthly thirty-minute call led by the co-chairs, tightly managed and ending early or on time. In-person gatherings were scheduled once or twice a year either as a social or training event or to share critical information. Creating clear communication, delivering on promises and authentically celebrating committee members' contributions leads to overall success in managing and achieving a campaign committee that's up to the challenge.

You can never leave footprints that last if you are always walking on tiptoe.

– Leymah Gbowee

Moonshots Can Experience Turbulence

Halfway into the capital campaign, in the summer of 2016, my husband Barney found out he had lung cancer. Within weeks he had his upper right lobe removed. At one point, both Jan and Barney were at the same healthcare facility receiving their respective cancer treatments and exchanging texts to check up on each other. His recovery would take six to eight weeks. The best way I was able to focus on my priority—Barney—while also keeping the campaign moving forward was to not talk about his struggles at work. By doing so, I could better manage the situations at home and office. My caring team graciously obliged. This experience made it painfully obvious to me that taking on a massive endeavor, such as a $55 million campaign, requires strong support from your family and work family.

As we closed our second year of the campaign, nearly $40 million of the $55 million had been raised, bringing us close to the forecasted goals with support from a wide array of donors such as Alliance Data, ClubCorp and the Moody Foundation, among others. The campaign was transitioning from the "silent phase" to the "public phase," with a February 17, 2017, tented event on 13.1 acres in Plano, our soon-to-be site for the new 230,000-square-foot distribution center called the Perot Family Campus. Fundraisers had their collective foot on the pedal to secure the final $600,000 of the forecasted $40 million in preparation to announce it at the big event. It was like playing three-dimensional chess. Fundraising team leads Courtney, Erin, Lauren and I checked in daily to get updates on critical gifts in the pipeline. The research team was continually adding new names. And, at the same time, we were behind in our annual fund goals.

This is where the art of fundraising enters. How do you secure a "Yes!" with intentionality, grace and patience? If any of those qualifiers are not in play, relationships can fade and supporters can walk away. In the final days, two gifts totaling $600,000 were confirmed, and because we knew each donor had worked extremely hard to confirm their gift in time for our announcement, we included them in the event's recognition remarks. Stewarding these two longtime relationships with authenticity and intentionality contributed to their "Yes!" in the final hours of our silent phase.

The "Going Public" event was executed flawlessly by the marketing and philanthropy teams. The weather was beautiful and the turnout strong. Jan had passed away a month prior, and this was the moment to acknowledge her significant achievements and memory. Her family, along with the board, the campaign co-chairs and committee, founders, supporters and volunteers filled the tent. Inspirational messages and tributes to Jan were shared as we celebrated her vision for a hunger-free North Texas.

At the conclusion, a new supporter came up to Board Chair-elect Anurag Jain and Interim CEO Simon Powell and handed them an envelope containing a $1 million check.

"I didn't want to take away from today's program so I waited until the end," she said as the contents were revealed. Anurag and Simon erupted with surprise, joy and gratitude for this transformational gift and honor. As I watched from across the tent, I witnessed the unadulterated joy that comes from sharing. As a fundraiser, those are the priceless memories that sustain you during the difficult and challenging times.

With this family's gift, we landed squarely at $41 million and *only* had to secure the final $14 million in the next ten-and-a-half months. Our pipeline's projected value well exceeded the $14 million needed. If we only received 50 percent of what had been qualified, we would hit our goal. What I'd soon learn is that nothing is certain until it is in ink—or at least pencil. A good lesson for a natural born optimist.

Over and over, I'd assure Jan, then Interim CEO Simon Powell, the executive team, Board Chairs Tom Black and, later, Anurag Jain, and board members that we would finish and on time. So what gave me that undying assurance?

First, I am a positive person. Jan was also optimistic, so combined we conjured all sorts of things into reality.

Second, I had a deep-seated drive to achieve this for the organization, for Jan and for those who would benefit: our partner agencies and those seeking a place at America's table.

Third, we had the best co-chairs in Pam and John Beckert. They were continually engaged, securing commitments wherever they saw an opening. Along with the Beckerts, I always knew our Board Chair Tom Black and Chair-elect Anurag Jain were there for me.

And finally, *I had the best team ever.* Smart, collaborative, loyal, hardworking and equally driven. They were dedicated to achieving *both* the capital campaign by January 2018 and the annual fund goal of $17.9 million by the following June 2018. Many fine individuals had come and gone over the years, yet it seemed as if all the stars aligned to bring this group of talented leaders together for this historic journey. I am in awe of what each one contributed.

Our vice president of human resources had created strong programs for recruiting, developing and recognizing both seasoned and emerging leaders and staff. CMP (Career Management Partners) had been hired by Jan five years before to help strengthen the executive team, and President Joe Frodsham's work was paying off.

The strength and health of any team can be seen during times of high stress and risk.

In July 2017, Trisha Cunningham was named president and CEO of NTFB from a vast array of qualified candidates. Retired after an impressive thirty-year career with Texas Instruments, she was now seeking her second career, which she referred to as "Trisha 2.0." As TI's former chief citizenship officer, she was well known among Texas nonprofit, corporate and community leaders. While we had met years before when NTFB was seeking TI's support, we had gotten to know each other better during the Leadership Texas class of 2010.

Trisha's arrival came at no better time. In the final months, she secured several six- and seven-figure gifts, ensuring the campaign's success. A brilliant strategist, she had quickly "learned" NTFB.

At the end of my NTFB journey, and fresh off the success of the capital campaign, I finished boxing up my office. I reflected on how I had worked with some remarkable, transformational servant leaders: Tom Quigley, Jan and Trisha. Moreover, some exceptional humans had mentored me along the way—my parents, Ruben Esquivel, Jack Phifer and Tom Quigley, along with a longtime friend, Lois Golbeck.

Moonshots x 2: Leadership by Two Catalyzed NTFB Growth
Joe Frodsham, President, CMP

When reminiscing about Jan, I have often heard Colleen say, *"I worked with, and for, the Steve Jobs of nonprofit."* This is a fair comparison. Like Steve Jobs, Jan was an innovator and bold leader who grew an organization that lives and thrives after she departed. And, like Steve Jobs, Jan didn't do it alone.

Steve Jobs had Steve Wozniak, and together they transformed the world of personal computing when they founded Apple Computer. The two Steves had the same name, but they were very different. Jobs was the public face with clarity of vision and tenacity, and Wozniak was in the background operating as the technical mastermind. Together they transformed the world of personal computing. And neither Steve could have done it without the other.

This theme of two leaders is consistent with every growth story. Bill Gates needed Steve Ballmer to build Microsoft, Bernie Marcus and Arthur Blank needed each other to build Home Depot, and Larry Page and Sergey Brin needed each other to create Google.

And Jan needed Colleen to grow NTFB to what it is today. Together they have created a legacy that is feeding millions.

This need for each other was never more evident than in the fall of 2013. As a consultant working with the NTFB executive team, I had the opportunity to discuss talent issues with Jan on a regular basis. In discussing the capital campaign and goal of $55 million, she said flatly, *"I need Colleen to lead the capital campaign. We won't get there without her."* With all her success, Jan had the humility and self-awareness to know she had a complementary leader in Colleen.

Moonshots x 2: Leadership by Two Catalyzed NTFB Growth
Joe Frodsham, President, CMP

Both Jan and Colleen knew they also needed strong leadership and talent across the organization. They engaged CMP as a talent development partner and embraced pre-hire assessment, team development and individual coaching solutions. NTFB got the right people on the bus.

Jan and Colleen have taught us that when two leaders are aligned with innovation, self-awareness and bold moves, the world will organize to their cause.

www.careermp.com

Jan's Impact on Public Support, Distributed Pounds, Volunteer Impact

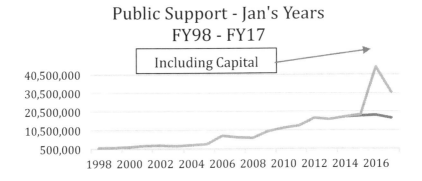

Public Support - Jan's Years
FY98 - FY17

Including Capital

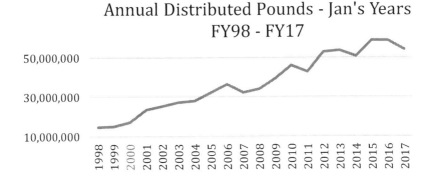

Annual Distributed Pounds - Jan's Years
FY98 - FY17

Annual Volunteer Hours - Jan's Years
FY03 - FY17
(no data on FY98 - FY02)

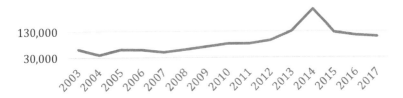

NTFB's Moonshot Growth and Impact

2002+	Grassroots startup; rapid operational growth; fertile soil for launching cause marketing and fundraising programs. Challenging times to build and retain the right team equipped for high growth. Nonetheless, an exciting place to work.
2003	Significant growth in direct response revenue due to new vendor's customized, integrated storytelling approach (Brad Cecil & Associates); began a disciplined focus on marketing with a team of one (me). The Lovell Group provided pro bono PR.
2005	First year to invest in a paid media holiday campaign, which every year since has generated significant year-over-year revenue increases (Year 1 agency: Moroch; Year 2+: RSW Creative).
2005–2007	First capital campaign to fund the renovation of the warehouse to increase efficiencies. Raised $4.5 million—more than the $4.2 million goal.
2009–2011	Launched three-year branded strategic plan, *Close the Gap*, to increase distribution from 26 million meals to 50 million. During this time, public support increased by 105 percent.
Holiday 2010	Paid holiday media campaign increased revenue by 22 percent YoY.
Holiday 2011	Paid holiday campaign increased revenue by 35 percent YoY.
2012–2014	Launched three-year branded strategic plan, *Rethink Hunger*, providing healthier, smarter and stronger solutions to end hunger. During this time public support increased by 37 percent.

Chapter 3
The *Char Minars*: Building Your Foundation for Good and Greatness

In a moment, I'll share with you the four key principles that drove the Food Bank's brand and resulting impact. First, I want to explain the reasoning behind the principles of *Char Minars* via a quick virtual trip to India.

Many of India's historic architectural structures have four towers, or pillars, girding the central building, which could be a fort, tomb or palace. "Char" means four and "Minars" refers to pillars. The Char Minars have a unique significance in the Indian culture, not only as a design principle, but also as a metaphor for building something of lasting meaning and value. The Taj Mahal is the most famous of these edifices, opened in 1648 as the mausoleum for Queen Mumtaz Mahal, who died while giving birth to her fourteenth child. Her husband, Shah Jahan, was so grief-stricken that he built this jewel-encrusted wonder of the world as an expression of his love for Mumtaz.

Char Minars is a useful frame for understanding the structure that built and strengthened NTFB's brand, resulting in a **588 percent increase in fundraising between 2004–2017**. Below are the Char Minars (or *four pillars*) for achieving transformational growth:

Minar # 1:	Right role, right place, right purpose.
Minar # 2:	Lead the right team (paid, unpaid).
Minar # 3:	Create the right value proposition. Then, deliver.
Minar # 4:	Think big. Today's issues demand it.

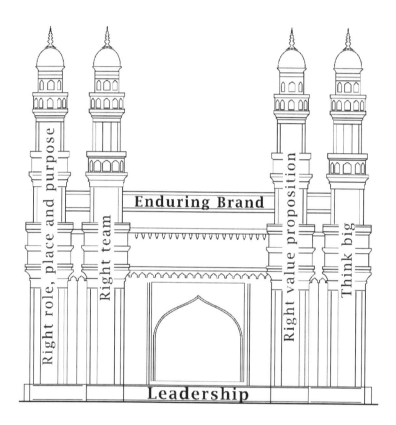

Minar #1: Right role, right place, right purpose.

Selecting the right cause for you is paramount. It is what connects your operating system with the mission and the hard work that awaits you. If there isn't alignment, success will be elusive. Don't let money or ego drive decisions. Dig deep inside yourself, seek guidance from your gurus and think with a clear head. Believe from the inside out.

Nonprofit work is not easy. You probably already know that, but it does bear repeating. Resources and compensation are tight, and you'll wear multiple hats. Building a brand is exhausting and requires a disciplined approach. Achieving ambitious goals can be difficult without a dedicated and trained team. However, what makes it worthwhile is knowing, at the end of a brutal day or week, that you have helped make life better for others.

Researching causes and organizations, their industry ranking, history, staff, board leadership (current and past) and financial stability will direct you to the best cause and organization for you. Use online tools like Charity Navigator, 990s, media coverage, blog postings and social media platforms. Talk with people who are employed by or partner with the organization. Sign up to volunteer or tour so you can have an experience akin to a mystery shopper. Dogged persistence with research will pay off.

Know what size sandbox you want. When I started my quest for meaning at the age of 35, I already knew I wanted to have a role in making a significant impact with core human needs, so the offer to serve as editor of a faith publication or executive director of a beloved Dallas cultural center was not appealing. Be cautious about moving too fast or allowing external or ethereal forces to influence you. Make sure you have inputs from confidants and mentors of various generations. Your decision to invest your energy with a particular organization will impact all the most critical aspects of your life, since most of us end up spending more waking hours with those at work than with the ones we love. Know your truths and what will make you sing. As Carl Jung said, "Our unconscious is the key to our life pursuits."

In my final year with Leadership Network in Dallas, a sizeable LA-based megachurch was aggressively recruiting me to join their leadership team to develop their global digital outreach. Of course, I was flattered. While I had concerns about the long-distance aspect and difference in our theologies, my ego was driving this conversation. Suddenly, the opportunity with the North Texas Food Bank accelerated, and I accepted their offer. As I reflected on all the time and energy invested in the megachurch recruitment phase, I realized I had not acknowledged the red flags waving madly inside me. I would not have been successful without living in that community and being fully invested in their culture and beliefs. Both they and I dodged a holy bullet.

Personal Application #7

What are your abiding principles? Survey a close friend/partner/spouse and a work colleague and have them candidly share with you what they perceive as your abiding principles. Are your actions and career aligned? If they aren't, what can you do to change?

Leadership by Two: Find the Right Leader for You

I am my best when my leader is visionary, passionate, smart, collaborative, operates with integrity and gives me space. That describes Tom, Jan and Trisha. On the innovation bell curve, Jan was a true innovator. I am an early adopter. That made for great "leadership by two."

Minar #2: Lead the right team (paid, unpaid).

Build small and grow smart. Whether creating your brand team or fundraising initiatives, it's vital that the foundation and structure be well thought out and robust. Once the first year or cycle is complete, adjust and scale. Otherwise, the house of sticks will fall.

Invest in having the right people on the team. Hiring quickly and accepting second choices are never worth it. Plan an interview process that places candidates in different environments. For example, at the Food Bank we'd give warehouse tours. You'd be surprised what you learn when you're not sitting across a table looking at each other. I recall our COO Paul Wunderlich reporting back to me after a tour with a fundraising candidate that they had held the door open for him, a gracious gesture indicating thoughtfulness and an attention to etiquette, both important features of relationship building. On another occasion during an interview, the candidate didn't ask any questions during the tour.

He just listened. The lack of curiosity and ability to converse raised a red flag. Create an interview team of diverse staff, thinkers and talents. You may be surprised with what they recognize that eludes you.

Focus on the mission; it will get you through the dark times. I had a four-year period, which I call "my dark years," during which public support increased from $6 million to $12 million, yet I faced some of my most significant challenges. It was 2010 to 2013. NTFB did not have professional HR services to provide recruitment, retention and recognition services. The compensation plan was outdated and under market for an organization our size. Other large food banks and peer nonprofits were in the same situation, so we had few models to emulate. We did not have the team and talent needed to fully execute the NTFB vision for marketing and fundraising to accomplish. Other key departments were poorly led and lacked collaboration. I felt like we were on an island, and many days I wanted to resign. While there were a few highly dedicated managers on my team, they were stretched thin, and their teams were less developed, causing the managers to cover, dive in and play multiple roles. It was a stressful time, and unfortunately, it put a strain on my relationship with Jan. I felt that Jan's trust in me was in question, causing even greater stress for me, and probably for my team. However, underneath the challenge and tension, I believe Jan and I had a reservoir of experience, caring and commitment to each other that kept us together. Moreover, I was still committed to the mission of NTFB.

Fortunately, in 2013 the tide changed.

As NTFB grew, and the complexity of our operations increased, we needed to add more strategic HR support. Jan hired NTFB's first vice president-level human resources expert, Belinda Bracey. With her arrival came a full complement of services that significantly improved the recruitment, hiring, development and retention of our talent. In retrospect, Jan wished she had hired this level of strategic HR support five years prior.

The most difficult thing is the decision to act, the rest is merely tenacity. The fears are paper tigers. You can do anything you decide to do. You can act to change and control your life; and the procedure, the process is its own reward.

– Amelia Earhart

Key Strategies That Built Our Winning Teams (Paid and Unpaid)

- **Communicate culture to attract and retain talent.** Millennials, who are on the cusp of being the most significant labor market, are in no small measure driven by purpose and impact. Inventory your external communications channels, digital and otherwise. How are you reaching your intended audiences, such as millennials, and are your messages customized for each group? What does your "Careers" web page say about your organizational culture? If it's bland, redesign it so it's a marketing beacon for the kinds of talent you are seeking. Include testimonials by third parties and use images, audio and video, focusing on all types of diversity.

- **Invest in professional development and recognition to retain talent.** Even with limited budgets, there are a wealth of pro bono options that offer employees professional development and recognition opportunities. Leverage your volunteers, board and corporate supporters to provide training, mentoring and other learning experiences as in-kind gifts. Create an annual Leadership Institute that provides leadership development to high performers. Leverage social media platforms to recognize exemplary team members. In your 360-degree partnership proposals presented to corporate prospects, request some intellectual capital and in-kind services in place of, or in addition to, financial support. This could be a professional development opportunity for *their* associates.

- **Share the podium, or step aside for another.** Build trust with your team members; give them space to spread their wings and soar. This is a journey, not something that happens in a snap. It's earned. Provide timely, clear and helpful counsel. A strong leader and active manager will have the self-confidence and wisdom to either share the moment or step aside to allow a protégé the opportunity. Remember, you cannot and should not do it all. (*Courtney, thank you.*)

Minar #3: Create the right value proposition. Then, deliver.

A rigorous focus on marketing creates enduring brands. Building a brand requires a disciplined approach over time. Being a nonprofit that no one knew, we said yes to everyone, regardless of what they wanted to do. We were customer service oriented and made sure no one left without being thanked and told what impact he or she had made. If a small tire shop wanted to do a food drive, we made sure they received the collection boxes even if we had to drive them over. Equally important were the large corporations. In my first five years, my team was one to five people in size, so we wore multiple hats. I was on fire and loved my work. Jan was always supportive of my ideas, and it seemed to me like I never "turned my NTFB button off." It didn't matter if I was at work or I was off duty, I was always looking for prospects to catch in my net. Certainly, that was good for the Food Bank, but eventually I did hit a wall.

Barney and I were driving to his university's local alumni chapter event where we were to watch a championship game. He remarked in the car that the event would afford me lots of opportunity to pitch NTFB. After a few moments of silence, I replied with an uncharacteristically direct tone. "I don't want to talk about the Food Bank here. Don't tell anyone where I work."

He was surprised, but being a supportive spouse and knowing me well, he obliged. I had a relaxing time watching the game with minimal interaction with others. I needed to be alone.

On Monday, Jan popped into my office and sat down. It was late afternoon and the place was quieting down. I shared with her what I had experienced over the weekend. She stared at me with her big blue eyes, and then nodded her head empathetically. I believe she, too, realized that to be strong for the long haul, one must take time to exhale, refuel and unplug. And be good to oneself.

As public support grew in response to our organizational goals, we had to be more strategic. No longer could our mantra be "say yes to everyone." Certainly we believed that and needed everyone to help with the mission, but the way we managed the business changed because our staff resources were still tight. We created savvy, engaging and user-friendly marketing toolkits and posted them online. When a company inquired about support, we would direct them to the online toolbox. As our flank of gift officers grew, we implemented a portfolio system where each officer was responsible for seventy to one hundred and twenty relationships, and had distinct annual fundraising goals for each. Others managed first-time and mid-level donors, direct response and our unique fundraising programs. We were even fortunate enough to hire a research analyst who produced profiles that played a direct role in our ability to cultivate, steward and close larger and larger gifts from individuals, corporations, foundations and civic organizations.

In the early years, people viewed hunger as an issue tied to homelessness, when in fact most of those at pantry doors were the working poor, 40 percent of whom had a permanent address.

Hunger was no longer an emergency situation, but something families, children and seniors faced month after month. Wages were not keeping up with the cost of living, and the cycle of poverty was hard to break. The face of hunger now looked like us. Only 8 to 10 percent of the food from the Food Bank went to shelters; most went to pantries serving working, low-income families, children and seniors. So, how does one shift misconceptions held by the public and civic leaders so they understand that hunger is a threat to economic strength? It was clear to me that we needed to recalibrate our messaging from the big funnel to a more strategic approach to help people understand how issues of a working wage, affordable housing and lack of nutritious foods all threaten the gleaming North Texas skyline, crowded with building cranes. We needed to reach corporate and faith leaders, elected officials and the workforce first. If we did that well, those employees would take the message of hunger home and mobilize their families, friends, neighbors, and faith, civic and educational circles.

Eight Factors that Create an Enduring Brand:

1. **Understand your organization's current reputation among donors, non-donors and the public. What's the perception of your cause? Do people understand what you do?** Invest in professional market research by finding the best firm and negotiating a three-year agreement. That way you'll see by year three if you've moved the needle. Keep the quantitative

and qualitative strategies consistent over the three years. Budget permitting, include a focus group of randomly selected significant donors and prospects.

2. **Know your donor profile.** Analyze your financial supporters and volunteers by gift range and retention, and know their profiles (age, household income, homeownership, gender, marital status, ZIP codes, etc.). Do the same for online donors; you may find they are younger and have a higher income bracket. This data will drive the work you do in marketing, communicating, direct mail strategy, event strategy and more. To build a major donor program, seek out existing and new luxury markets and build partnerships with them. Understand who the community and opinion leaders are. Values and fundraising preferences for millennials and Generation Zs will be radically different for these groups. Generally, members of Generation Z are tech-savvy, pragmatic, open minded and individualistic, but also socially responsible. Facebook and cable television may not appeal to them.

3. **Make sure your brand, collateral and communication channels reflect organizational values, mission and need.** This applies to everything from your online presence, lobby, volunteer experience, events and campaigns, and staff. Does your marketing convey that you are family friendly, yet when people attend events, campaigns or volunteer they get a different vibe? Do you emphasize the efficiency of your

operations, yet a facility appears to be in disarray and unclean, and the parking lot hard to find? Are you proud to emphasize inclusivity and respect for all, but the staff and the community sense or know otherwise? Do you post your data privacy policies on all digital and print communications? Conduct an annual online survey with a diverse array of supporters and ask for anonymous feedback. Keep the survey brief. Once solutions to issues raised are identified, use the opportunity to communicate with your supporters that improvements are underway and how their voice matters.

4. **Identify targeted emerging markets and set measurable engagement goals.** With input from your team, donor database and marketplace, identify four or five emerging markets to focus on for three to five fiscal years. These are target groups that have a high propensity for supporting your cause, are locally robust and have discretionary income. NTFB focused on six emerging markets over the previous five years: all were high wealth, high density and guided by the core values of philanthropy, family values and social justice. The Food Bank focused on deepening relationships with the Indian-American, LGBTQA+ and Jewish communities, in addition to residents in several high-income ZIP codes.

      When the organization decided to expand its awareness in a northern suburb, we added those ZIP codes to our emerging market goals. Measurable goals tied to engagement and funds and first-time donors were set. Once our team understood each of these communities, there was a collective effort to build critical relationships within them, be engaged, obtain media coverage in their preferred news sources and raise funds. Because of this targeted focus, new opportunities arose to engage more firmly with the communities. Bar and bat mitzvahs generated financial and food support, NTFB sponsored a truck in the Dallas Pride Parade, and Resounding Harmony dedicated concerts over three years to NTFB. The Indian-American Council launched, introducing dozens of new families to NTFB within the first month. Year after year, the number of new donors and board members from the targeted ZIP codes slowly increased. This low-cost strategy was paying off.

5. **Never forget you have competition—time.** People, no matter how loyal, will never have enough time to do all on their to-do list. So, how do you build a sense of urgency via your communications and brand so people of all stripes, including your target markets, will keep your cause near the top of their priority list? Competition is not just the other charity down the block. It's much bigger than that.

6. **Invest in building strong media relationships.** NTFB's media relationships extended well beyond the mainstream editors and reporters of print, radio, TV and digital media. There was a constant push to build relationships with trade media focused on retailers, farmers, food manufacturers, policy makers, faith

entities and even private school alumni groups. By widening our lenses, we had an abundance of stories to pitch strategically, and we found the media receptive to our calls. After the *Wall Street Journal* ran a story on the Food Bank, I received a call wanting to know what it would cost for a tractor-trailer load of frozen chicken. "$100,000," I replied. The caller then mailed in a check from his out-of-state address. With a one-person communications team, we soon recruited a volunteer writer to serve as our roving reporter, who wrote content for our website and digital publications and submitted copy-ready stories to smaller community publications throughout North Texas.

7. **You won't have a second chance to make a first impression.** Ensure your facilities and all your incoming channels operate with efficiency, professionalism and a customer service mind-set. Recruit seasoned, trusted volunteers to be mystery shoppers for each of your incoming channels. Ask six to ten volunteers to sign up for a tour or volunteer shift, request info on an event or seek a callback from a specific department. Ask for feedback on their whole 360-degree experience. For example, when they drove onto your organization's property, was it easy to find with or without GPS? Did it have available and well-marked parking and ease of entry into the lobby? Was the front desk staff welcoming and their workspace tidy? Was the free literature up to date and relevant? Were the restrooms clean? Was content on public bulletin boards current and

enticing? Was it easy to navigate the phone tree system, and were their calls returned in a timely way? Was there a sense of energy among the other volunteers and staff? This feedback will be priceless for two reasons: one, it will help retain or improve the customer experience, which translates into greater public support, and two, it will give you some great "kudos" to convey back to staff.

8. **Patience pays off.** An iconic, global corporation recently relocated to Plano, Texas, and, of course, the community, region and state were thrilled, ceremoniously rolling out the "welcome mat." Plano's Mayor Harry LaRosiliere introduced them to the Food Bank and, soon after, they indicated an interest in bringing a group of managers to volunteer and tour our distribution center. For many, it would be their first time to meet relocated colleagues from other national offices. The joy and effervescence were palpable that day. It was the first time I experienced their well-known corporate culture of respect and balance, which we captured in a video gifted a week later. Over the following months, we got to know their key communications leaders and a congenial relationship grew. A top executive joined the board, and other leadership opportunities to join our Young Professionals group were extended. Employees participated in events, holiday food drives and volunteer experiences. As the second year of the relationship ended, we had still held off on asking for financial support. I firmly believe that when relationships are built with

open hearts, mutual respect and exemplary customer service, all things happen for good. As we approached the final year of the capital campaign, the company invited us to present a 360-degree partnership opportunity that included opportunities for financial, in-kind and volunteer support. Because the relationship was built with patience, authenticity, gratitude and professionalism, the company, in short measure, announced a seven-figure gift to the capital campaign. This corporation models for the world how to make good happen. By continuing to focus on strategically developing key corporate relationships with patience and a 360-degree mind-set, your organization's brand will exponentially grow.

Moonshot Leadership: Observations of Successful North Texas Food Bank Marketing
Jack Phifer, Chief Marketing Officer, Moroch (retired)

The success of a leader must ultimately be viewed through the lens of the success of that organization. The success of the organization and the team is the legacy of the leader. The group, and what they do next, is the long-term scorecard of the leader.

In marketing, we have all observed that:

- Some companies, brands and organizations become great.
- Some could be.
- Some rise to greatness, but it's short-lived, and they disappear or diminish to irrelevance.

Success is available to many, but elusive to most, especially on a sustained basis. This is primarily due to not understanding the core principles and operating behaviors that create sustained success. These are grounded in high character and high competency. NTFB has had both.

NTFB marketing has understood that you can't always be the biggest, but you can strive to be the best every day. It's not the size of the budget, but the size of the ambition and heart.

NTFB marketing never operated like a nonprofit looking for "assistance." Rather, it always behaved like a blue-chip brand that just happened to be a nonprofit, and thus was "attracting." Instead of essentially saying "help us," they said, "join us."

They communicated the feeling of, "We are doing important work in the right way, and we'd love to have you join us." This applied to all the partners and companies that they dealt with. It was something we

Moonshot Leadership: Observations of Successful North Texas Food Bank Marketing (Cont.)

could feel. The proof of the above can be found in the family of partners and the accomplishments of NTFB.

All these qualities and habits were evident from our first meeting with Colleen and her team.

- **Her team brought a genuine enthusiasm for the space**, and that made us, as an agency, want to "lean in" even further.

- **There was a "clarity of understanding"** by Jan and Colleen— for the mission and the target.

- **As a result, there was an efficiency of decision making** by NTFB management—and that drove energy and momentum.

- **Wanting to reach for better**—and then better beyond that— wanting an "A" game in all areas.

- **Colleen was "outward looking"**—benchmarking her practices and marketing against not just food banks, but the most successful and iconic nonprofits.

- **She and Jan were not afraid of "Big Audacious Goals."** Whether it was things like the backpack program, number of meals served or capital campaigns, they set their own versions of the Apollo moon landing and reached them.

- **The balance of team and individual accountability.** In every successful team, there is also the understanding that everyone has a valuable role—and the team only wins if everyone does their individual job.

All of this led the Food Bank to being confident, but never arrogant. Never assuming success or overplaying its hand, like some brands do. Reaching for the stars while keeping their feet firmly on the ground.

Moonshot Leadership: Observations of Successful North Texas Food Bank Marketing (Cont.)

In short, the Food Bank did something special by not thinking that they were "special."

What creates success? Someone once said, "alignment," or knowing what you like and are good at, and then finding someone who wants THAT!

By that measure, Colleen and the Food Bank finding one another makes her one of the most successful people I have ever worked with.

www.moroch.com

Minar #4: Think big. Today's issues demand it.

We know this. The issues facing our planet, nation and community are massive. It can be overwhelming. The media inflow is never-ending and we often feel whiplashed.

Personal Application #8

Using the ideas shared above, host a marketing idea session led by a volunteer marketing professional. Invite various staff who interface with supporters and the public. Draw concentric circles, starting with the organization's mission and core goals in the bull's-eye. In the next ring, list your internal and external stakeholders, plus emerging target markets. In the third ring, include all the ways you provide "an experience" to them, from volunteerism, serving on the board, attending events, holding fundraisers, making a donation, participating in a speaking engagement, etc. Now, brainstorm the many ways the organization communicates the various messages, from media stories, social media, telephone, website, donor meets and more.

What new channels are missing? Are some of the ways you're communicating not reaching the target audience? Are the stories you're pitching to industry trade publications also shining the light on a corporate donor? Where are the areas for improvement and reinvention? What do you need to stop doing?

A focus on building and nourishing your organization's brand will help keep the base of the donor pyramid strong and growing.

However, to raise significantly increased amounts, creating and growing programs like these are vital:

1) Major donor program
2) Special volunteer-led, high-value initiatives (Pam Beckert's Letter Writing Campaign; Jingle Bell Mistletoe Campaign)
3) Affinity Groups (Young Professionals, Indian-American Council, a board alumni group and Kids Against Hunger)
4) Cause marketing (DFW Restaurant Week, point-of-sale campaigns)
5) Anniversary campaigns to mark milestones from five years to twenty-five years and up
6) Paid holiday media campaigns
7) Volunteer experience(s) for various demographics, including corporations who host their clients and vendors
8) Planned giving programs
9) Board recruitment, orientation and fundraising plans

Find Your Mayor Harry

One of the biggest change-makers in the Food Bank's thirty-five years has been its relationship with Plano's Mayor Harry LaRosiliere. Named as one of the "Safest Cities in America" and "Best Run Cities in America" by Law Street Media and 24/7 Wall Street respectively, Plano is admired

Mayor Harry LaRosiliere, Plano, Texas

as a great place to live and work. Passionate about ending hunger in Plano, Mayor Harry reached out to Jan and me at the start of his term as mayor. From that moment, game-changer shifts started happening. Mayor Harry helped raise nearly $5 million to support

Mayor Harry's annual holiday food drive in action

hunger relief, $2 million for the weekend backpack program for chronically hungry Plano ISD children, and nearly $3 million for the capital campaign.

His encouragement and guidance were invaluable when NTFB sought to relocate its campus to Plano. He founded the popular annual Thanksgiving and Peanut Butter Drives and introduced countless corporate leaders to NTFB. Time and again, Mayor Harry introduced leaders, global corporations and change-makers to the Food Bank, and addressed hunger in his State of the City annual address. To serve him and these new relationships well, a designated senior gift officer managed the business and relationships. (*Thank you, Jessica.*) Without a doubt, Mayor Harry's visionary leadership played a key role in ensuring that North Texans have a seat at the table. Any organization seeking transformational change needs to **find their Mayor Harry**.

Personal Application #9

Who in your community is your "Mayor Harry"? What next steps do you need to take to make this new transformational relationship happen?

Tracy LaRosiliere, Mayor Harry, and me

Ana Meade of Toyota North America, Mayor Harry, me, and Courtney Bagot of NTFB

Epilogue
Find Your Shine

As I said earlier, I don't have a magical potion to hand to you, but only my experiences and learnings from this remarkable, sometimes bumpy but ever so rewarding journey. What I did realize after burying my second parent is that I would not get a chance to flip over my hourglass of sand for a second go-round.

This is it.

I can either stay the course, safe and beige, or listen to that inner voice that is challenging me to explore and find my "Here!"

I'm glad I chose the latter. I genuinely hope you do too.

hands folded, deep bow

Find your shine.

Colleen

I've always liked small surprise treats. Consider this your "surprise piece of chocolate" after a hearty meal. Years after this experience occurred, I realized that my journey to feed the hungry started at the tender age of 5. Enjoy!

Chacha Nehru Liked Kheel

Dr. Rev. Hendrix A. Townsley,
my father

It was Chacha Prime Minister Nehru's birthday in 1958. We had just come to Delhi from South India and I thought it would be a thrill for our two girls, Kay and Colleen, to meet him personally. We started good and early for we lived in Old Delhi. The girls wanted to honor him with something more than just flower garlands. So they took the specially strung variety made by

Nehru with my sister K and me, 1958

stringing kheel (puffed rice) grains in several strands.

At the gate we were due for a shock. "I am sorry," said the attendant, "but there are to be no garlands presented to the Prime Minister personally. They are all to be placed on this table and he will see them when he walks by." With a wave of his hand he indicated a large table in the center of the lawn which had a "mountain" of garlands collected on it. "Oh, but these are special garlands," I said, "and will get spoiled in the midst of all those flowers." The forlorn look on Colleen's face must have touched the heart of the attendant, so he waved us by and let us take our

117

garlands in our hands, while others were piling theirs higher and higher on the table.

Well, good enough. We were past our first hurdle but what would the Prime Minister say when we tried to garland him? This was the question now. "Chacha Nehru!" "Uncle Nehru," cried all the children near the front door, for just then he emerged from his house. Then began a sweet little battle. For the attendants had not just taken the garlands from the children. In place of the garlands, they had given each child a handful of rose petals to shower upon the beloved Prime Minister. The shower turned into a running battle. The children would pelt him and he, being supplied by his attendants, would return the "fire." Around the massive circles he went in a storm of petals.

As he neared us, he threw his flowers on our girls and they threw some back, then summoning up all their courage for the critical moment of garlanding. "Sir," I asked, "our girls have brought some very special garlands which we thought would get spoiled in the pile of flowers on the table. Might they place theirs on you?" His reply was immediate, "Why sure. Thank goodness someone brought me something good to eat."

And with that he pulled off a few of the grains and ate them as he received the garland! The girls were thrilled. They had met, garlanded and fed the Prime Minister!

Then, he posed for a photo and dug the rose petals out of Kay's neck. What a thrill.

Acknowledgements

These pages would not have been possible without the unconditional love from my family—Barney; Rob, Midori, Lewis; Jessica, Britt, Zeke; Dylan, Rayna, and Lillian; and my brilliant guiding light sister K;

Jan Pruitt, for all that followed after that Chinese lunch;

Trisha Cunningham, for your friendship and for exuberantly propelling us over the finish line;

My dear friend Andie Hill, for saying yes to Stuart and NTFB;

My awe-inspiring, best-in-class North Texas Food Bank team, who planted the flag on *our* Everest;

Erin Fincher, a remarkable leader and friend who still holds the record for securing the single largest NTFB gift ever; thank you for your commitment;

My heroes (forever), Pam and John Beckert;

Board chairs and friends Tom and Bridget Black, Anurag and Gunjan Jain, and board members (1982–2018);

Liz Minyard Lokey and Kathy Hall, for your inspired lives and friendship;

Jay Pack, for your friendship, especially as we approached the finish line;

NTFB's dedicated capital campaign committee;

Brad Cecil, the best capital campaign counsel;

Maryanne Piña-Frodsham and Joe Frodsham, my inspiring and talented partners in making good happen;

Brad Cecil & Associates, RSW Creative and The Lovell Group for shining the light on the journey;

Mentors Ruben Esquivel, Lois Golbeck, Jack Phifer and Tom Quigley;

Retta Miller and Shannon Zmud Teicher of Jackson Walker for your caring guidance;

Kim Iltis for your decades of friendship and creative magic;

Lee J. Colan and Julie Davis-Colan for creating NTFB's Leadership Institute and helping build bench strength;

For your gifts of time and input—Lydia Chase, Steve Chase, Jeanne Clark, Sydney Frodsham, Vince Golbeck, Chris Greissinger, Ruth Morrison Hakeem, Jane Hardin, Lauren Banta Holloway, Sayeda Mahler, Vickie Mathews, Talia Sampson, Steve Shaw, Cindy Wenban and Paul Wunderlich; and

Erica Yaeger, for accepting the baton and beginning your own moonshot journey.

As an early adopter, if I jump on the first spaceship for Mars,
I know who to take with me.

–Colleen

About the Author

Colleen Townsley Brinkmann, CFRE, is senior consultant, Purpose-Driven Strategy and Brand, for CMP where she brings thirty years of nonprofit executive and management experience. Colleen culminated her sixteen-year career with the North Texas Food Bank by leading its historic $55 million *Stop Hunger Build Hope* capital campaign and raising more than $110 million between 2015–2018 for operations and capital needs. Under her leadership, the Food Bank's public support increased by 588 percent, from $2.6 million in 2004 to $17.9 million in 2018. She traces her passion for social justice and moonshot treks to her upbringing in India where she lived with her remarkable parents and sister in a hundred-year-old stone bungalow on the edge of a forest filled with dancing peacocks. Colleen is an artist, writer and storyteller and strives to "live life in neon." She and her husband live in Dallas and Sacramento.

Moonshot Leadership
www.moonshotleaders.com

My greatest honor—first recipient of the Jan Pruitt Legacy Award, 2017.
(L-R) Trisha Cunningham, Jessica Eileen Hager, me, Barney Brinkmann,
Natalie Pruitt, and Charles Pruitt

Photography and other visual credits: Barney Brinkmann, Rachel DeLira, Brad Cecil & Associates, Hendrix Townsley, North Texas Food Bank, RSW Creative.

The CMP Difference

CMP is a talent and transition firm in the business of developing people and organizations across the full talent life cycle—from executive search and leadership development, to deep assessment, coaching, and career transition support. In doing so, we combine our decades of experience with a contemporary approach to building people and teams. We marry the art and science of talent and prediction to provide individuals and organizations with a unique competitive advantage.

Beyond what we do, *Moonshot Leadership* is connected to our "why." CMP exists to positively impact the individuals and communities we serve. Partnering with Colleen to document her story and share her learnings in *Moonshot Leadership* was an honor. We are confident that it will positively impact the people who read *Moonshot Leadership*, and the Purpose-Driven organizations and communities who apply the principles. Thank you, Colleen!

As someone who is reading *Moonshot Leadership*, we suspect you care about being effective and having an impact. If there is anything we can do for you, your people, or your organization, please do not hesitate to contact us.

www.careermp.com

Made in the USA
Columbia, SC
16 November 2018